TRANSITIONS OF

HOPE

Using the **Power** of the **Mind** to Replace **Fear** with **Love** to Navigate **Life's Challenges**

MARYANN ROEFARO

Transitions of Hope
Maryann Roefaro

First Printing, 2025

ISBN-13: 978-1-968401-18-4 print edition
ISBN-13: 978-1-968401-19-1 ebook edition

Printed in the United States of America

Cover design and layout by impactbookdesigns.com

Waterside Publishing
2055 Oxford Ave
Cardiff, CA 92007
www.waterside.com

CONTENTS

Dedication

This book is lovingly dedicated to the Trinity of Women who molded the formation of my character and who motivated my desire to be good and do good work.

My mother, **Angela Maria Roefaro**

My mother's mother, my Gramma, **Leah Mirante Roefaro**

My mother's sister, my aunt, **Rose Roefaro Casatelli**

I am forever grateful for their eternal love, unwavering support and tender companionship we shared and still share—past, present and future.

Acknowledgments

One of the finest decisions made before my entry to planet earth was the selection of my parents, Angela Marie Roefaro and Renato James Roefaro Sr., and the agreements we committed to fulfill for my lifetime. The love and influence they provided, and still provide from the other side, is the primary reason I am the individual I am today. There are no words to express the depths of my love and gratitude to them.

I can never forget to thank my two brothers, Louis Roefaro and Renato Roefaro Jr. for their unwavering support and love throughout all the chapters of my life. Deepest love and gratitude to my grandma, Leah Mirante Roefaro, for she was the strongest and most resilient woman I have ever known. An abundance of gratitude and love for my stepmom, Carol Roefaro. Her love and admiration have always been great motivators and sources of strength for me.

Love and immense gratitude to my daughters, Casey A. Prietti and Angela M. Warne. My love for them goes beyond any earthy words or sentiments. True love comes again in the form of their children, Anthony Renato Prietti and Oliver Michael Warne. Your Mimi loves you beyond measure, and I'll never leave you and will always provide guidance and support regardless of what form my spirit takes. All my love to a few more who call me Mimi, in order of appearance: Declan, Joey, Lena, and Islay Carranti.

This book has been greatly influenced by my former husband and the father of my children, Dale H. Franz. Dale died of metastatic pancreatic cancer in February of 2024. Our eight-month journey together taught me a great deal about true love, soul connections, forgiveness, and the malleability of hope. Ending as we began, the best of friends, was a reflection of the relationships and love we shared through many lifetimes. Our souls will always be connected through love.

Speaking of precious soul connections through lifetimes,

immense love and thanks to my husband, Tom Carranti. Challenge only allows the heart to grow fonder—it's been a ride worth sharing!

Love forever to my dogs Mille and Bella. The place you hold in my heart and soul is one of the most precious, for you both are honest examples of unconditional love.

Deepest gratitude to Bill Gladstone who transitioned in 2023. His support brought my hopes to be an author to life. Special thanks to Ken Fraser who designed the cover of this book and to Josh Freel and the wonderful staff at Waterside.

We are really nothing without those who love us—so thanks to all of you who have loved and supported me—you know how special you are to me!

Chapter One

Introduction

As with everything in life, our perspectives about people, places, and things are a reflection from the inside out. Our relationship with hope is dependent upon the same criteria that affect every aspect of our lives. It is completely dependent upon the relationship we have with ourselves.

We are all unique products of our physical, emotional, mental, and spiritual environment—past, present, and future. As we grow from an infant, we don't have the capacity to understand the world, and we depend on those around us we believe we can trust. Our belief comes from the proof we experience in the form of food, shelter, protection, communication, guidance, and hopefully a lot of love and affection. As the years pass, we accept that what these trustworthy people tell us is true, and we begin to assimilate their beliefs and patterns of thought into our own. They are our role models, and we watch them very carefully. We learn to speak by repeating their words, and we learn what's important by watching them in every encounter to which we are exposed. By the time we are mature enough to engage our independent thinking, we have blended our past into our conscious and subconscious minds. It is likely that much of our opinion about ourselves is very much a reflection of what we've heard others say to us or about us. As we mature and learn through a multitude of sources, we continue to weave the tapestry of our being with intertwined threads that we've gathered along the way. Our sense of self and our values and priorities are likely mixed together with those whom we have trusted and loved since our infancy. Although the individuals who assisted in the formation of the framework of this growth may not have always had the best intentions, philosophies, or attributes, the mind of an infant or child does not possess the ability or maturity to understand how to sift through that information to seek the truths that are paramount to healthy development. Everyone is a product of their environment—positive or negative, good or bad.

Life can be stressful and filled with challenges that come in many varieties, sizes, shapes, colors, and flavors. Some of these challenges motivate us to be the best version of ourselves and to work relentlessly to achieve our hopes and dreams, and others test our internal fortitude at maximum capacity and often result in self-sabotage because the tools to navigate discomfort have never been developed. Some challenges seem insurmountable and some seem trivial, but to each person it's all relative, and stress elicits physical, emotional, mental, and spiritual challenges that only love and self-mastery can overcome.

The number and examples of the challenges we face on a minute-to-minute basis here on earth are too numerous to count and too expansive to articulate. What we do know, however, is that everyone processes information about our external world differently, based upon the lens through which they view life. A lens that has been developed over millennia and reflects not only what is external and visible, but also that which resides on the inside, often obscured by clutter and coupled with information of which we only have small parts of the complete dataset. The only opportunity to obtain the entire dataset is death—death of the human body and release of the soul to reunite with our higher self or spirit in the magnificent sea of love and Oneness. Here, in this unfathomable vibration of love, we have access to our entire story, our former lifetimes, our soul interactions and agreements while in physical form, our co-created plans, and the dataset of our existence. (Much more on this later.)

One of the most important gifts a parent, guardian, or caregiver can give a child, in addition to love and unwavering support, is resilience. Regardless of how much we love someone, it's imperative for them to make their own mistakes, learn how to cope and solve problems, and deal with the alleged unfairness, challenges, and sadness that life brings. I say alleged because we assume that life is unfair and challenged by what is brought forth in our view and perceptions. Resilience is born from optimism and hope, knowing that everything will work out, and in every challenge rests opportunity. It's helpful for parents or caregivers to provide an environment for young minds to witness the role of optimism, positivity, and a sense of confidence, faith, and strength to get through life's challenges. As I said before, all of us—regardless of how brilliant, educated, wise, and cultured we are—only have a piece of the dataset before us. We don't often understand we have co-created a plan for spiritual evolution and soul growth that includes karmic rebalance and purposeful placement of obstacles in our path to overcome any weaknesses or faults we have determined we want to strengthen or resolve within the lifetime we have chosen on earth.

Hope places light in front of our challenges so the shadows can move behind us. Within the shadows, however, resides opportunity. Opportunity to become the best versions of ourselves and to help make the world a better place. Hope and resilience are powerful tools that allow our light and love to absorb, transform, and eliminate any darkness.

One of the most difficult challenges in life is loss or fear of loss. Loss can occur in many instances because it includes so many more circumstances than death. Never minimizing the permanent ache of losing someone we loved beyond measure, death, if not understood, can create a genuine challenge to carry on with life. Dealing with having or caring for an individual with an acute or chronic disease can also test every fiber of resilience one possesses. Within this suffering, we often feel guilty that death is the only fate that can resolve this struggle.

We are creatures immersed in an earthly vat filled with more opportunities for stress and struggle than for peace, because humanity has created it that way. These are expectations that have been set forth by those who have come before us, and we continue to allow history to be on repeat. We often lament about yesterday and fear for tomorrow, thereby minimizing the potential joy of today. We complicate our lives by breathing life into situations that don't actually exist. We throw obstacles into our lives without acknowledging our role in chaos. When we are not mindful of our thoughts and self-talk, we often don't realize our level of self-sabotage in the creation of our world. Many have thoughts of unworthiness and can't accept joy for fear that the other shoe will drop any minute or once again. So many are searching and striving for work-life balance but will not step off the hamster wheel for fear of loss. Many muddle through Monday through Friday blues, living for the weekends and wishing time away. Some love their jobs but are exhausted by the rat race and feel trapped. They still wish their week away because the demands of living can be exhausting, and there never seems to be enough time . . . treading water as fast as they can to stay ahead of mortgage payments, credit card debt, and other bills in a world with increasing needs, wants, and costs. There are some who have a ton of money and never have to worry about having spare change. However, some of those rich in revenue are poor in life because although they have a ton of money, they have realized that money can't buy what they are looking for, and they can feel lost among the luxury—lost while trying to identify and cope with the void. There are those who cannot live within the structure that humankind has created, and I have to say some of the most precious and beautiful souls I have known live within this matrix of struggle. They try to escape in any way they can to release themselves from the burdens of earthly life. Some people may perceive, from the limited view they possess, that these types of individuals are "losers" who can't get their act together. Perhaps at some level of consciousness those individuals who struggle know what awaits on the other side, and their souls lament for home, without their conscious awareness. Regardless of how hard they try, some individuals just can't get it "together" as societal norms would dictate. Some even take their own lives to relieve their pain, and others self-anesthetize in their quest to eliminate the forces of earthy life. The examples are endless.

I should mention that some of the national and global issues seem overwhelmingly frightening, heartbreaking, and truly necessitate our resilience and hope. Our political structure is flawed and unsustainable to create honest change and improvement for the lives of their constituency. Healthcare and payment systems are broken and unsustainable. The healthcare spending curve in the US continues to accelerate at unconscionable levels that will subsequently necessitate increased premiums or reduced benefits. There will be a day when the expense is so dramatically skewed from affordability that the system will either need dramatic change or it will break. Those who can help fix it are voices that will never be heard, as they are those who have spent a lifetime in the trenches and not in an ivory tower or governmental edifice. The tough decisions that need to be made, such as the elimination of for-profit insurance companies, Pharmacy Benefit Managers, and insurance-owned specialty pharmacies to name a few, are unlikely because of power and money. It's becoming more difficult for every sized and shaped healthcare entity to render the kind of care we expect in the United States. We have the greatest costs with the some of the worst clinical outcomes and life expectancies. In the US we experience the highest healthcare costs per capita and rank fortieth in overall mortality. It's getting close to impossible to accommodate the needs of our elderly with insufficient funds, unfunded mandates, poor reimbursement, or the potential loss of a life's savings. Global issues are voluminous, and it seems like humanity hasn't learned any lessons from our past. The energy that creates war cannot be the energy that allows for resolution and peace. In all instances, the energy that creates a problem will never be the energy that solves it. Love is the answer. A type of love for global peace and tolerance that requires the ego, narcissistic predispositions, and hidden agendas to be dissolved. It's also difficult to trust any type of news broadcast or media outlet because we live among waves of deception. Politicians are rarely altruistic anymore, and those who yell loudest often hide their secrets within the chaos and layers of inefficiency in our government.

Life's challenges force us to find hope and develop a sustainable plan for our sanity, well-being, or happiness.

We all know, however, if we are realistic, that the target of hope is one that is in constant motion. When we allow love to move that target instead of fear, we have the freedom and capacity to cope—to be resilient—and to play the cards we are dealt with grace and fortitude.

Regardless of our individual situations, level of education, socioeconomic status, or state of health, none of us get through life unscathed. Life is stressful and filled with challenges. An element of resilience that allows us to navigate these challenges is having hope, and our level of resilience is often related to our ability to generate hope for ourselves and others. This journey of hope has many variations, and it makes sense that it's a moving target because realistically, life changes moment by moment. Everyone deals with issues and solves problems based upon the relationship they have with themselves, and thus how they perceive the challenges of life on earth. A person's journey of hope may have similarities to other people's journeys, but it's always an individual, inside job—and that can be difficult for family and close friends to accept. Based on the never-ending changes in circumstances that present themselves from moment to moment, *Transitions of Hope* is a book that can help us to understand ourselves and the situations that life presents at a more profound, deeper level and help people cope with the challenges of life through love and the realistic, moving target of hope. It is *my hope* that you will find this information helpful and that you will inquire within to understand what's going on inside and clear some of the clutter that is obscuring the joy-filled life of which we all desire and are worthy. Please note I did not say create an easy life—nobody ever said a joy-filled life is an easy life, but with self-mastery or self-realization, life can evolve with a greater component of ease because our perspective about challenge changes. The goal is to find joy among the muck that life throws at us so we aren't affected by the minute-to-minute changes in our environment or the circumstances we cannot change, but we can work above that, with the best part of ourselves, to create the life we wish to have.

Chapter Two

The Slope of Hope

As I write this book, I recently retired as the CEO of the largest physician-owned, independent cancer center in Central New York. As of 2025, it is the last purely independent physician-owned cancer practice in New York State that is not a member of any large super group or hospital system. During my tenure of twenty-three years, we served hundreds of thousands of people, many of whom I had the privilege to know or get to know and love. I developed some special relationships with so many patients throughout those years, some who beat cancer and many who did not. Those who died taught me more about living than I could have imagined. I always believed walking with someone in their end-of-life journey was one of the greatest privileges we could witness. I shared that thought with our staff as often as I could because they became beacons of hope every day to hundreds of patients and their caregivers as our patients and their families dealt with a magnitude of diverse challenges. Having had such an incredible exposure to cancer patients, I tried to help create an environment that would support the minds, bodies, and spirits of those dealing with cancer. When I saw a genuine need for the staff, patients, or caregivers, I did my best to create the conditions to meet those needs. I was the cofounder and as of this writing am still the President of the Board of

Directors of CancerConnects, Inc., an organization dedicated to facilitating the cancer journey for cancer patients in our community. CancerConnects provides mentoring opportunities for newly diagnosed and recurrent cancer patients; vouchers for free integrative therapies like Reiki, massage, and acupuncture; and financial assistance through stipends for co-pays, secondary insurance policies, mortgage payments, daycare, car payments, and other similar financial assistance. This organization has proven to be a precious jewel in our community serving hundreds of cancer patients and dispersing millions of dollars to our Central New York community over the last decade. It was important for me to support community foundations that served our patients and others. Of note, I spent twelve years on our community's hospice board, nine years on the CNY Komen Foundation board, twenty-two years on the Syracuse Home/McHarrie Life board (independent living, assisted living, memory care, and long-term care facility), twenty-three years on the Multiple Sclerosis Resources of CNY board, and I've been on other cancer and non-cancer related boards in my community. Recently, I joined the Francis House board—a Central New York shelter caring for sixteen people and their families at end-of-life. Throughout my life, I've witnessed the fragility of the human body and the indestructible spirit and resilience of humanity. As early as seven years old, when my mother had brain surgery for a benign tumor and had to relearn how to walk and talk due to the severing of one of her cranial nerves, I was a participant in the healing journey of people motivated to restore their composition. During my career, I witnessed intelligent, educated, beautiful people, including prominent community leaders, struggle to remain whole or accept their transformation into shells of their former selves. Cancer and debilitating chronic diseases show no favoritism or prejudice, and many are affected in one way or another by these cruel challenges. In my years as a CEO of this cancer practice, I've been a part of tragedy and celebration. I've been in healthcare all my life—starting with candy striping at fourteen years old!

During my time as CEO, some patients maintained a positive attitude throughout their entire cancer journey and some did not. Some patients and families rejoiced in the miracle of cure or remission, and some allowed their loved ones to transition freely to a realm of love, free from pain and suffering. Some patients and families accepted that death was imminent and navigated the end with love and grace. Some patients and families remained in denial and deprived themselves of a precious and loving send-off. Some families united and some families divided. Some patients and families bathe themselves in love and others bathe themselves in anger and resentment. Regardless of circumstances and disease progression, everyone has the freedom of choice and can create the environment they desire.

For some patients, from the start, they were consumed with negativity and denial, and that energy permeated their journey. Those who maintained a positive attitude and were convinced they could get through treatment happy and whole did just that. Others truly believed they'd be sick, and it was going to be a painful and cruel journey. In both cases, their self-fulfilling prophecies usually came to fruition. As it turns out, and the physicians and staff will agree, attitude is one of the most important tools in the arsenal of healing. The power of our minds should never be underestimated because real power resides within the thoughts that create our existence. It isn't fruitful to wish for a particular situation or outcome, as wishing doesn't usually do the job. A person can, however, create the conditions for that wish to come true. Some family members or caregivers were angry and fearful of losing their loved one and put forth great pressure for more and more treatments. Sometimes I'd walk through infusion and I would see beautiful people who were frail, feeble, and often skeletal in appearance. It always saddened me because I knew that their infusion time could be spent in precious moments, immersed in love, instead of getting futile treatments. Most family members or caregivers put the patient first and supported every decision they made—whether they agreed with them or not. One of the elements of life that cancer can't take away is a patient's ability to choose— to be in control of their journey and not swimming in guilt because they are disappointing someone they love.

Some patients witnessed miracles in their lives and subsequently felt that having cancer was a life-altering gift. Some patients had benign disease and were thankful to graduate from the practice or be told to come to the office only if needed. Some patients suffered horrendously, went through rigorous treatments, and eventually celebrated to have cancer in their rearview mirror, forever grateful for the cure or remission. Some patients fought with everything they had, exhausted every possibility for resolution of the cancer, but died due to the progression of their disease or the side effects that manifested from having treatments. Some patients died kicking and screaming, still unable to accept their fate. Some patients were at peace, and they and their families accepted death with love and strength. Sometimes, a patient presented who was thrilled to end their treatments as the exhaustion and stress of the journey was no longer something they wanted to entertain, and the decision to cease treatments and enter palliative care was a huge relief. They were relieved to cease treatments, live in peace, and die with an open mind and heart—they were in a state of serenity to have their souls released into the vibration of love, excited about the possibilities and love that awaited.

How we live is imperative to how we die. One of the most difficult journeys of hope is watching somebody you love struggle with a disease or illness. Caregivers are often exhausted from the stress of care, from the roller coaster of ups and downs, and from the commitment of resources they may or may not have. Hope really floats on this winding and undulating road, and there's a myriad of emotions that cascade on a daily basis. When someone we love dies, if we **don't** understand that they are vibrating at a different frequency, in a form that does not include their earthy bodies but can be with us and see us and not miss a trick, it can render an individual paralyzed to continue to live on this earth with that magnitude of loss.

My daughters and I spent fifteen days with my former husband at Francis House prior to his death. Francis House is a beautiful home where hospice can serve people who are dying, most of whom live alone or whose family needs help caring for them at end-of-life. Dale, my former husband and father of my children, had been diagnosed with stage 4 pancreatic cancer eight months before his admission to hospice and Francis House. Even through the years we were separated, Dale always meant the world to me. We met and started dating in college at nineteen years old, and he was one of the most brilliant and wonderful humans I have ever known. He was blessed to have beaten stomach cancer twenty-one years prior to this new diagnosis. In those years, he was able to see his daughters grow up, graduate with master's degrees, and begin successful and happy careers. He was able to walk both girls down the aisle when they married, and he met his first grandchild while in the physical, and he was in the delivery room for the second, not taking up as much room as he was in spirit. During that eight-month journey, he and I were as tight as we were in college, where we became best friends for the second time in our lives. We spent a bit over twenty years dating and married, and we spent a bit over twenty years divorced. In this lifetime, although our life plans would find us divorced, it was evident to both of us, especially at the end of his physical existence, that our soul journey was one of millennia. True love is forever, and comes in a variety of forms. My daughters and I had many precious moments with him, but as with all caregivers, our broken hearts were further broken to see him waste away to nothing, struggling for sanity and breath. We were with him in every decision he made, whether it was agreeable to us or not. He fought like a remarkable warrior and died in peace, surrounded by love, as we all encouraged him to embrace his transition to freedom and pure love. He landed on the other side well, welcomed by his mom, who had passed years before, and today I can tell you that he is beyond happy. We communicate frequently, and I know he has found his place with love and peace. His loss, however, still stings for us as naturally we all miss his physical presence, skills, and sense of humor.

Our journey of hope throughout his pancreatic cancer journey proceeded through many iterations of hope. When he was first diagnosed, we were filled with hope that he would beat this cancer—at least for a few years. He was a fighter through rigorous and difficult treatments, and as his cancer tumor markers continued to decrease, we continued to be filled with greater hope that perhaps we truly would have more years together. The slope of hope was high.

Shortly after the last cycle of the first eight rounds of

chemo, he could not eat, and he barely drank. Hydration through infusion was a savior many times, but regardless, his inability to eat and constant nausea began to render the deterioration of his body. Irrespective of our begging him to eat—a common act among caregivers and their loved ones struggling with a diagnosis and the treatment of cancer—he had no desire to eat, and the malnutrition and dehydration took a serious toll on his body and quality of life. As it turns out, the pancreatic cancer had caused a fistula at the jejunum, likely causing the nausea and complicating the situation. Since Dale had had his stomach removed from his first cancer, his anatomy precipitated significantly more challenges than if he had been a patient with a stomach. When he planned on coming to my house for Christmas dinner at four o'clock in the evening and it was 4:15 with no word, I knew something was wrong. Our level of hope had taken a beating by now as we were consumed with sadness and concern through this roller coaster of fatigue, malnutrition, and dehydration—a familiar story to many. Our slope of hope had also been on a roller coaster, and the slope was declining rapidly because our hopes for a short-term or long-term reprieve from this cancer journey with any level of quality time was slipping away. Christmas evening, when I arrived at his home, he was sporting the concentration camp look, and when we looked at each other, our eyes said it all—we knew we had to do something. We were off to the ER the next day, and he was admitted. After a couple of days of parenteral nutrition and hydration, it was determined that a G-tube (gastrointestinal tube that allows nutrition to enter the body without eating) may provide nourishment to assist him to better health. Our slope of hope took a sharp turn up, and once again, we were hopeful for the resolution of his malnutrition and weakness and more time on earth with a better quality of life. He was discharged and still went into the office to work whenever he could. He was a director of pharmacy at Crouse Hospital, an acute care hospital where he had worked for over forty years. Work meant a great deal to him, and he pushed himself to continue to work during treatments, trying desperately to maintain some semblance of normalcy. It's important to all cancer patients that they control any facet of their lives that they are able. Work meant sustaining life to him, and regardless of how he felt, he pushed and pushed. Thankfully, his family, coworkers, and employer supported his choices. We all waited for him to get stronger so he could continue chemo as by this time, he had not had any chemo treatments for about eight weeks due to his severe weakness and malnutrition issues. We all waited for his physical presentation to turn the corner and improve. Unfortunately, the corner never turned in the direction we were all hoping for—a situation that millions of caregivers experience every day around the globe. Dale's G-tube was getting plugged frequently, perhaps because of the pancreatic cancer itself, and more health challenges continued to arise. He still couldn't drink, and because he had not received chemo in some time, his cancer tumor markers started to increase, indicating progression of disease. Our aggregate slope of hope took a downward turn as the reality of death was not only coming into clearer view, but it was also presenting as a better option. Dale and I talked very honestly about the road ahead and the quality of life that awaited him and all of us. We knew that everyone, including the oncology medical team, had done everything possible, and we were at the end of the earthly road as we had exhausted all possibilities to create a life that anyone would want to live. When we decided that Dale had done everything he could—that he had fought the best fight possible—it was time to change course.

Now, our slope of hope increased profoundly, but the goal and light at the end of the tunnel were much different from the last time a slope of this elevation existed. The endgame was now very different. Our hope of a loving, peaceful, and pain-free transition was all that mattered to us. We had to create the conditions for what we desired to come to fruition, and cancer was no longer in charge, calling the shots. **We were in charge**—our family—planning the way to a beautiful death of a physical vehicle so his soul could be released into the purest vibration of love. We all were acutely aware of the absence of death—simply an existence in a different frequency of vibration—and this is what makes the loss of a loved one hopeful and bearable.

My children had grown up and lived in an environment where death was only a transition from the physical world to the spiritual realm. My daughters were acutely aware of my continual communication with my mother, as well as her unwavering love and support throughout my life and theirs, from the other side. We sang "Happy Birthday" to her each year when the girls were young, and we kept her alive and well in our home when the girls were in their formative stages. There were always extraordinary examples of proof of her presence, and I taught my girls to understand that death truly did not exist and to be aware of these precious tiny miracles. They grew up acutely aware of signs from the other side. Our way of life had prepared our family for Dale's transition. Every one of us believed to our core that Dale would not miss a trick when he died, and there was no question he would be able continue to be a part of all our lives. We had precious moments of talking, laughing, and sharing that had not taken place as a family for many years. Our family had time to heal anything and everything that could prevent Dale's new journey from being fabulous and our lives from having any guilt. There would be no words that had not been said by the time he took his last breath.

Those who are not proponents of the Death with Dignity movement or physician-assisted death would underscore the beauty of our journey and what we would have missed had we used that level of assistance. However, every element of that journey would have been experienced with the exception of the last two days, which everyone wishes we could forget. In those last two days, there was no talking, laughing, or sharing. If Dale had had a choice, on day twelve, we would have had our celebration of life, and he would have drifted off to the other side, relaxed, eyes and mouth closed, while we all embraced him and professed our love. He was still coherent and skilled enough to feed himself the sorbet that would have allowed him to fall asleep and drift to the spirit world. He and I talked about it, and he wanted me to support the legalization of physician-assisted death in New York State when he transitioned, and he committed to help from the other side. As of August 2025, the bill is awaiting signature by the governor, and I'm hoping New York will become the thirteenth state allowing legalized physician-assisted death. In my career, having a lot of exposure to end-of-life issues, I have been told many times, death is not always a painless and peaceful transition. Some people drift off peacefully, others suffocate and gasp for air, and others writhe in pain because the perfect concoction of drugs could not be administered. With Dale, the lapse between breaths in those last two days were hopefully only painful for us to watch. As his skin began to be mottled and purple, his breath labored, pulse high, blood pressure diminishing, we waited. His eyes partly open, his mouth open like it was gasping for air, we knew the end was near. The last two days were extremely difficult to witness as we had no control over the situation other than to ensure that the prescribed end-of-life drugs were administered. He finally transitioned in the early morning of day fifteen, eyes and mouth partly open. I can't say it was a pretty site, but we were happy he was free.

At the end, during his end-of-life journey, our slope of hope was high. We were filled with great hope, not for life, but for death. Dale's journey of hope had many twists and turns, but as we all talked about the gifts of the other side, all his newfound skills he'd develop and the profound experience of love that awaited, he lovingly accepted his new adventure with great hope. The kind of hope we started with was very different from the kind of hope we ended this journey with, but nonetheless, love and positive thinking paved the way, and the elevation of the slope of hope was as high as it was at the start. The slope of hope was just comprised of different goals.

Physician-assisted death is only controversial because humans insist on imparting their perceptions and ideologies on others. If we were created in the image of love, to reside on a planet built on the foundation of free will, why do people think that it's OK to remove choice in the most personal decisions that only affect the people making those decisions? As I said, we don't ever have the full dataset of information that allows us to understand the many nuances in people's lives. We know that there is a universal mandate to rebalance that which positively and negatively affects the whole—this is called karma. We never have to worry about getting revenge because the universal mandate of rebalance is real. The *how* is none of our business, but the karmic rebalance is a guarantee. Make no mistake, we reap what we sow, and we will discuss this concept in much greater detail in forthcoming chapters.

Death with dignity or physician-assisted death at end-of-life, when a terminal diagnosis indicates that transition to the other side is imminent, is a very personal decision. As of August 2025, medical aid in dying is legal in twelve US states: Oregon; Washington; Montana; Vermont; California; Colorado; Washington, DC; Hawaii; New Jersey; Maine; New Mexico; and Delaware. The laws surrounding this usually coincide with a hospice admission whereby the individual is terminally ill with a prognosis of six months or fewer to live and requires mental competence and multiple medical confirmations. When looking at the data in the states that allow this kind of peaceful and pain-free transition, some people never self-administer the drugs and die on their own, as just having the option alleviates fear and needless suffering. At the end, a person who elected this opportunity may not have needed assistance in their transition, but just having the option allowed for a peaceful and fearless death for both the deceased and their caregivers or family members. Those people who decide to have physician assistance in death drift off to a peaceful death with the people and scenery they desire and should never be judged. What's most important, I strongly believe, is the availability of the option for all people. If an individual's personal convictions or beliefs prohibit them from this type of assistance at death, so be it, they will never have to expose themselves to this option. I've watched a few people I loved with all my heart die, and none were interested in prolonged suffering, pain, and fear for themselves or those they loved.

I have watched a terminal diagnosis cause deterioration of the body, cell by cell, organ by organ, breath by breath—it renders everyone helpless and can offer an inhumane exit where death is not peaceful or pretty. I have heard stories about caregivers and loved ones watching a horrific death as the end-of-life/palliative drugs were not sufficient to allow a peaceful transition. It can and does happen, even with the best of intentions. We can live without food for a rather long time, but we can't live without water for very long. Watching someone dehydrate and starve to death is very difficult. Within the ten years that this law was proposed in New York, I asked numerous cancer patients how they felt about it. Most were not interested in suffering and had more anxiety about the process of dying than the destination. The majority were not afraid of death but were extremely anxious about the process and level of pain, anxiety or suffering they may need to endure.

It is inhumane to dictate suffering because some feel strongly that suffering is a mandate on planet earth. A God without human characteristic who only loves does not wish their offspring suffering. There are people who believe suffering has great value. There is always an expression of love and extension of energetic signals that correspond with sacrifices such as pain, and they can bring about change. The malleability and growth of the soul that suffering renders, however, is unique to each person and is part and parcel to the co-created plan and purpose for soul growth set forth prior to earth entry and during a physical lifetime. Heaven is a vibration of love and light where levels of consciousness are created by the frequencies of love that correspond to the level of soul growth associated with each individual and will provide the optimal environment for continued love, support, and ascension of the soul. Heaven meets a spirit at the level of consciousness or vibration that corresponds to their evolution of soul. (More about this later.)

This world will be a more loving and peaceful place when that peace and love resides within each individual person. We are all connected to each other and every-thing that vibrates with life. If we could only understand when we hurt others, we hurt ourselves and vice versa, we may understand our ability to effectuate profound chang-es within families, communities, and governments. Spirit can inspire us, but they can't control us. Nobody has the ability to control another as earth is a free will planet. Hav-ing said that, there are people who allow others to control them as they give away their incredible power from within. Everyone can create their own thoughts and thereby cre-ate their own life and as such, to a significant extent, the circumstances of their existence.

When people transition out of their earthy, physical bod-ies, they hang around for a few days, close to their body and the people they love. For a short time, they still vibrate at a frequency that many of us can connect to who have an awareness of that capability. There are people who can easily communicate with anyone residing on the other side, regardless of time. These mediums are usually born with an ability to communicate with the dead and have this gift from an early age. Our loved ones often offer great insights and advice, as they have an eagle-eye view of life from their vantage point. Those on the other side can teach us a great deal about the opportunities that await.

With those I truly love and maintain an extremely close relationship with, our bond of love transcends this earthly plain, and our vibrations can sync to a level where com-munication becomes possible. I am in no way a medium who communicates with the dead. However, I am intuitive enough to be able to communicate with those I love. I need to be in the right state of consciousness to connect. This is typically a state of relaxation or surrender—as when I'm meditating or running. A person may find it unusual that running offers this state of consciousness, but it's one of the most effective ways for me to connect to spirit. Although my body is moving, my mind slows significantly, and my vibration can be easily altered after a few miles. One of the reasons I run is because in that state of being, I can clearly hear from the divine. As the years pass, practice has made it easier for me to pause, tune in, and listen without a lot of preparation.

We all navigate through different levels of consciousness throughout the day, every day. We daydream, drift, and often do something while we are not consciously paying attention. Driving home and don't recall how you got there? Driving home and you weren't supposed to go home? Those are two common examples of an altered state of consciousness. Meditation is not difficult, and you can practice while you sit, relax, and take deep breaths, visualizing a beautiful ocean, waves, blue sky, and so on. The spectrum of the levels of consciousness are from being highly aware and paying attention to every detail to falling asleep and dreaming! We will talk about our subconscious and superconscious minds (our higher selves) in later chapters.

We are all capable of altering our consciousness and connecting with spirit. It's like an intuition that comes from a different place in your head than your own thoughts. For example, I get my info from spirit from the right side of my head, a little above and behind my right ear. Often when I'm downloading and writing using their inspiration, that spot will get a bit sore—like it has overheated!

If you're interested in trying to decipher thoughts from your imagination versus spirit, you can perform this simple exercise. You can close your eyes and finish what I tell you with the thought *violets are blue*. Ready . . . Say this out loud, "Roses are red," . . . and then relax and think *violets are blue*. Do it repeatedly if necessary, and pay attention to the exact location in your head where your thoughts originated when you thought *violets are blue*. When you've determined the location in your head, just pay attention the next time you're meditating or praying. If you get a message from another place in your head, you'll know it's not your thoughts or your imagination. With practice, the location of your communication with spirit will become more defined and consistent, and you'll be able to acknowledge messages from spirit. With time, you can develop the confidence to trust these communications and believe that this type of intuition is not coming from your imagination. I was about thirty-eight years old when someone taught me this technique, and it cleared up confusion and self-doubt for me. Like any exercise or practice, the more you do it, the better you get at it. If you're worried about communication with beings that are not of the light or highly evolved—just set that rule/intention. Put the light of the Christ Consciousness around you and state that only that which is of love or high vibrations of light and divinity can communicate with you. The divine will protect you—all you need to do is ask and give thanks that your request has been answered.

My first introduction to this voice within my head was at age seven. My mother was having brain surgery, and I visited her in the hospital the evening before, along with my dad and my two brothers. As I look back, they must have made an exception for a seven-year-old during visiting hours because the situation was serious enough that she may not have lived through the surgery. That evening, I sat next to her on her hospital bed and asked what was happening. I wanted to know what was going to happen, and she made light of it, telling me that they were just cutting behind her ear, as she pointed to that area, and saying that it was no big deal. Of course, I had no reason to doubt what she was telling me; to my knowledge she never lied to me. A lesson—tell children the truth, regardless of how you think they'll assimilate the information or react to it. Lies are not helpful, and the energy of lies when left to linger over time have a negative effect on children and the home environment, whether anyone acknowledges it or not. Now I am positive that her intention, as was the intention of the other members of my family, was to protect me. They didn't want to scare me or make me worry. That's all well and good; however, the truth almost always comes out at some point in the future—and sometimes sooner rather than later. Like I said, keeping secrets changes the energy of a household. At some level of consciousness, children know something is not right, and that energy shift from the person/people who are keeping secrets often affects the daily life or the future of the people who are thought to be left in the dark.

My mother had a brain tumor the size of a golf ball. I'm not sure of the anatomical position of the tumor or what the scientific cell line was that differentiated it as I was too young to know or ask and my family was not healthcare oriented, so the specifics remain unknown to me. What I do know is that they had to cut at least one cranial nerve that had a lasting imprint, and the tumor was not cancerous, it was benign.

When we left the hospital and I was in bed for the night, my dad came into my bedroom. He asked me to include my mother in my nightly prayers, and he asked me to tell God that we were selfish and we didn't want him to take her to heaven but to leave her with us. I recall being confused. I did what he asked but I thought it was strange because she was just having a cut behind her ear. How could she die from that? I remember how much that uncertainly bothered me. As a reminder, I was seven!

The next day, my mother's mother—my beloved Gramma Leah was crying and saying the rosary most of the day. My uncle, my mother's brother, paced up and down the driveway for hours. Once again, I asked myself, *Really? All this for a cut behind her ear.* Please note that I still did not doubt that my mother was not telling me the truth. I thought my family was overreacting and kind of crazy. It's interesting that I believed my mother wholeheartedly and questioned everyone else's overreaction to the situation as I knew it to be—but then again, she was my world for the entire existence I had her in human form.

The great news: mom was out of surgery, and it was successful. She would be coming home soon. I'm not sure how long she was in the hospital, but the day she came home will be burned into my permanent memory for all the days of my life and probably beyond. She came home the Friday or Saturday before my First Holy Communion that occurred that Sunday—and that's how I remember. We had a party that day, and my father took 8 mm moving pictures to commemorate the event. So not only will I never forget what we both looked like, I can easily access the film that I had transferred to DVDs many years later.

The day she came home, there was a bit of commotion at my house. It was decided she would sleep in my brother's room. There were twin beds in there, and it would be easier for her convalescence. My brothers were thirteen and nineteen years old at the time. I can't recall where my older brother slept while my mom occupied his bed, and I can't recall if my other brother slept in his own bed in that room. Everything else I'm pretty clear about. When the car pulled into the driveway to help my mother out, my dad, grandmother, brothers, and uncle were all there. They wouldn't allow my help even if I asked, so I watched from my bedroom window. I saw a women get out of the car who I didn't know. She could hardly balance and walk, and she had no hair. Her hands and mouth moved in an uncoordinated fashion, and frankly, it scared the shit out of me. I threw myself under my bed, and there I remained for what seemed like hours—but I'm sure it wasn't.

I watched the feet walk in the hallway and pass my bedroom doorway. Someone was walking backward so they could hold onto my mother's arms to help her walk. I listened to the commotion in the next room while they all tried to get my mother settled. I remained under my bed, scared and too frightened to come out . . . until I heard the voice. It was the most loving, kind, and protective motherly voice. I'm still not certain exactly whose voice that was, but the one thing I'm certain of is that it was of a divine nature. Since I loved the Blessed Mother from the day I found out she existed, and my mother had a deep devotion to her with communication through her daily rosary, I wouldn't be surprised if the motherly voice was hers. This loving voice told me that everything was going to be all right, that my mother was the same mother I knew, and that she'd get better soon. She told me that I didn't have to be afraid, and I couldn't spend the rest of my life under my bed. It was short and sweet but to the point! I remember how natural the conversation felt—so much so that I think I must have had communications before, but I don't remember. I do recall saying OK, I would get out from under my bed.

Slowly, when the people scattered, I made it to the doorway of my brothers' room. My mom spotted me and smiled, and she told me, with her crooked mouth, that it was OK that I could come visit her. Soon after, I would spend lots of time helping my mother get back to a more operational state. Until she died, when she was tired, however, she would start walking with a slight limp, and her mouth would slant slightly. Other than that, she was strong, resilient, and the same person I always knew. The next seven years would be filled with a lot of love, sharing, and unwavering support. We shared everything, and we frequently talked about death or the absence thereof. She was really my first self-mastery guru. She was wise beyond measure, and she is the reason I am who I am today. She taught me things that other people or religions could have never done. She died seven years later when I was fourteen after several surgeries to remove a tumor that did not exist. Her actual cause of death was sepsis. The day of her death was the worst day of my life thus far, but the blessings from her divine presence, continued communication, and unconditional love and nurturing are too numerous to count. During my high school years, college, and career, there are too many instances to count where I thought, *How do people get through life without a dead mother?* She has taught me more about life than anyone I know, and I have often had inclinations about why her co-created plan would include an early death at fifty-three years old. There is always a reason for everything!

Chapter Three

Unconditional Love Is Being, Not Doing

As above so below. We begin our journey back home preparing for our arrival on planet earth. There are likely preparations for other destinations, but for the purposes of this book, we will stick with planet earth. It's important to understand these concepts as they are fundamental building blocks in the journey of hope as we try to understand, accept, and navigate life's challenges. Earth is a free will planet filled with opportunities for incredible spiritual evolution and soul growth. One of the most important purposes of our lives on earth can actually be viewed as a journey in reverse, for the purpose of every soul, using love as the navigator is to discover our way back to the beginning, where we were created from and by love. Acknowledging that we are spiritual beings who have chosen to have a temporary physical existence, we understand that everything on planet earth is temporary. There is a much closer connection between the spiritual side and the earth side than one may think. This connection is accessible to everyone and can provide a strong, supporting, and miraculous infrastructure of love and guidance if we acknowledge its existence and welcome the connection into our lives. This infrastructure is known by many names, heaven being one of them, but I commonly refer to it as the "other side." For this reverse journey, it's essential to have a relationship with our Creator and understand that we are created from love, the threads of which bind each and every one of us to each other. It's imperative to understand two facts: 1) heaven or the other side is not a place, it's a vibration; and 2) unconditional love is an act of being and not an act of doing. A good question to periodically ask ourselves, especially when we are at any kind of cross-road is, "What would unconditional love do?"

Being unconditional love does not mean that we condone bad behavior or that we have to love those who hurt us or others, as most of us would surely fail. It does not mean that we allow ourselves to be a doormat, walked upon by others. It does not mean that we must love those people who exhibit the characteristics of meanness, hatred, greed, anger, or deceit. It does not mean we have to love our enemies; it means we should try our best to respect their physical, emotional, mental, and spiritual reality, even if we cannot fathom maintaining their belief system. It means that we forgive them by sending love to the situations of which they are a part that seem to break our hearts and then let it go. It's important to understand that we only have an external view. We don't understand the difference these souls committed to make, regardless of what that commitment and purpose look like on earth. There are souls walking the planet who came to earth with a mission to be a "disrupter." These disrupters can be loved by some, hated by others. These disrupters may be extremely misunderstood, and the external presentation may be very different from accepted norms. It is often within tragedy that lives become closer and the love that binds people together becomes more evident. World challenges and global heartaches set up an environment of potential whereby it may become easier to fathom or understand our Oneness or connection with each other. We have no idea what the end game is for a life that, from the outside looking in, seems inhumane or horrible. We don't know the co-created plan or the reasons people do what they do; it is imperative to understand that everyone has a limited dataset, and no individual can possibly know the life of a soul, the soul contracts that were committed to, or the earthy plan that has been co-created for any lifetime. This includes the individuals themselves, which is why we often can't understand why the circumstances or challenges of our lives can be such a heavy lift. Before we come to earth, we select our parents and siblings as we mutually agree to our aggregate highest good for our earthly plan. We know our name before we are born. We make agreements with others to help them and have them help us navigate our lives to achieve those goals within our co-created plans. Many times, people cannot accept this fact, as they are certain they would never select the parents or siblings or challenges they were handed. The sole reason for this lack of acceptance is the lack of knowledge or awareness regarding the *why*, and earthly amnesia of the soul can take credit for that mandate. Amnesia is imperative if free will is to be successfully exercised. There are times when amnesia takes a back seat, as with prodigies who seem to be born with lifetimes worth of gifts, but otherwise it's a necessity. Suicide is never in a co-created plan, but because of free will, an individual can opt for that exit strategy. Negative ramifications of suicide do not exist for a soul when it arrives back home, as it's usually placed in a cocoon of love, kindness, and protection. Any kind of relegation to darkness or punishment because somebody ends their own life does not exist. The soul is usually in need of love and compassion to assist in the transition. It's important to acknowledge, however, that suicide does not remove the grief or suffering of the soul. Suicide provides a nonphysical, loving, and safe environment to continue the inside work to resolve whatever issues plagued the individual—but the escape that people may perceive does not exist. Mental, emotional, and spiritual dysfunctions or challenges need to be healed one way or another, on either side of the veil.

Soul and spirit are often used interchangeably, but they are different aspects of the self. Our soul has lived many lifetimes, and our soul represents the eternal energy and light that defines our being. This encompasses each of our unique personalities, the levels of consciousness we attain, and all the potential we have to make decisions and function within the form in which we reside. Our spirit is usually viewed as the divine, eternal aspects of our being. Our spirit is our higher self—that part of us that connects us with the collective consciousness, divinity, love, and Oneness. During a physical incarnation, our spirit maintains all the wisdom of our previous and in-between lives, and we can tap into that consciousness for guidance. Our spirits do not come to planet earth with amnesia and can therefore be an incredible guiding and loving force when we access that level of divinity within ourselves. The soul comes to earth having a spiritual experience within a physical or human vessel. The soul must experience amnesia so we can learn, redirect ourselves, make independent decisions, and try to navigate the world by accomplishing the objectives and goals set forth for ourselves when we developed our co-created plan in between earthly lifetimes. On earth, the soul does not recall our lifetimes of successes, failures, and co-created plans that have gone fulfilled or unfulfilled. The spirit is the divine aspect of ourselves and, at times, our soul or conscious awareness can acquire glimpses of the soul's journey and past lifetimes or begin to understand elements of our co-created plans. This allows our soul to evolve at more profound levels of consciousness to prepare us for our life review when we detach from our human vessel and return home. Our spirit is that part of us, while we inhabit our human vehicles that is connected to "all that is." Our spirit allows us to access our higher selves and collective consciousness of love, light, wisdom, and divine vibrations while we are alive. When our cord is cut for the second time—one at birth to our human mothers who gave us life and at the end when the cord is severed between our souls and our human bodies—the soul is free to unite with the spirt to continue its evolution of consciousness and love. This freedom allows for a life review and an understanding of the self and others that cannot be experienced until death. With death, once again, we gain access to our complete dataset and our souls continue to exist in infinitum on the other side, reunited with the ultimate consciousness of love and all the elements of our soul's existence from the past, present, and future. Aspects of our personality are therefore preserved. Many think when they die, they'll float as an entity who no longer has to work on healing the mental, emotional, and spiritual issues that may have plagued them and that their new, nonhuman existence will be perfect. Not true. We continue to work on any issue or baggage we've taken with us, and we continue to develop a higher vibration of love. If someone is a jerk, their jerk personality remains, and they will need to work on whatever can make them vibrate to a higher frequency of love, minimizing and losing the jerk tendencies when they die. The only thing we completely shed is any physical pain associated with being human—disease, suffering, soreness, blindness, deafness, chromosomal nondisjunction, and so on. Those elements of challenge are removed with the loss of the physical vessel. The soul and all the characteristics and components thereof remain. Sometimes it's difficult to understand things within our human perspectives, and I know this subtle, yet essential difference can be perplexing to the human mind. Suffice it to say, upon death, our wholeness of spirit understands our complete existence with all the data and information that resided outside our awareness on earth.

When the Bible was written in Aramaic, before it was translated several times before it was completed in English, the word for love that was used when they transcribed "love your enemies" was a different Aramaic word from the one used with "love your neighbor." When I studied a tiny bit of Aramaic (and I mean teeny tiny) many years ago, I learned that the word that was transcribed for "love your enemies" was more related to respect than to what we would understand or associate with love. In Aramaic, the vibration of words was very important, and there are nuances in that language, as with other languages, that are difficult to translate, especially into English. Being unconditional love means we accept that which we cannot truly understand or change, and we forgive those who neither have the eyes to see nor the ears to hear and therefore don't comprehend that they were created by love and therefore are love. Being unconditional love means that a level of respect is maintained for all life, especially people or communities or nations that may not acknowledge the Oneness of existence or each soul's purpose, or co-created plan. It means that we accept that regardless of how much we know, there is information that resides outside our scope of knowing and that we accept that our beliefs, regardless of how much we think they are accurate, can differ significantly from others, and acceptance, understanding, and tolerance is paramount. Being human, we see what is in front of us, and we perceive our reality through the lens through which we view all of life. A lens that is created by our truths and misgivings. We often have no idea of the purpose of our challenges, heartaches, heartbreaks, or celebrations, but hopefully we trust there is a reason. It is merely a lack of exposure or understanding that requires acceptance and surrender. There are also those who vibrate in a very dense and dark frequency, and their minds are not open to the light and love of the divine. They feel comfortable living in that density, and they may be closed to any injection of light or love. As unconditional love, we should consciously fill every void we find with our love. Love is the answer to just about every question we can query!

Being unconditional love **does** mean that all the negativity, war, hatred, violence, or genocide in this world can hurt and anger us to our core, but it allows us to understand that every soul is evolving to the place that is in accordance with their divine plan, and it's not our jobs to judge—our love will allow us to accept and do the best we can with what we and they are given. As I said, we think like humans, and we filter everything through our own lens. Missing the entire dataset, we often misunderstand or are confused by the tragedies of life because they make no sense to us. It's easy to love someone who meets all our criteria or expectations. If we try to love everyone unconditionally, we will surely fail, but if we understand that **we are unconditional love,** we will look at situations differently and accept that the only person we can control is ourselves, and loving ourselves is paramount to loving anyone or anything else. We create the conditions for our lives through our thoughts.

The reverse path home, to the beginning, is simple in

concept yet difficult to bring to fruition. Remembering our way back home has many obstacles on planet earth—the land of density. The first obstacle takes place with our first breath at birth—and the onset of amnesia. I think it's worth spending more time on this concept of amnesia. In this case, the amnesia of which I speak is amnesia upon birth that results in a situation in which we forget all we learned, experienced, studied, and accomplished from other lifetimes and while residing on the other side. Most of us don't recall our past lives and are unaware of the celebrations and challenges we've set forth before us on our new journey, as well as the reasons that go along with those events. Amnesia takes a bit of time to fully integrate itself into our conscious awareness. As a child grows, they get more domesticated with each passing day, and as a result they grow closer to the earthly side of thinking and further away from their divine side of being. Young toddlers often see those we love who have passed and spend time playing with them. As they grow and develop, they slowly slip away from the other side and become more like everybody else, fully embedded in living on the earth plane.

It's essential to understand why amnesia after human birth is so important. The existence of a fully functioning free will planet can only occur if the people have amnesia and are allowed to spiritually evolve through their own individual choices. Free will is the basic right given by the Creator to all souls. It's the right to be who you are and make choices that continually authenticate your truth. Life is in perpetual motion with a myriad of possibilities and options. Our choices in life provide evidence of our authentic self and our ability to think freely. Through choices, we give support to our lives, our love, and our truth. We are children of an all-loving Creator, not the children of conditions, events, or happenstance. Free will provides the freedom to remove boundaries created by circumstance. Limitations occur by the boundaries humans put in their path and place upon themselves. People can opt for the choices that lead them in any direction they desire, and these decisions may or may not be compatible with love. Everyone always has a choice. Even in the direst of circumstances, a person always has the freedom to think the way they want to think. Nobody can make somebody else think the way they want them to, but they sure can influence how they think, and especially how they think about themselves. When a person allows another to have that level of influence, they give away their power— the power of thought that can drive the direction of life, while love (or the lack thereof) creates the essence of a person's existence. Free will empowers a person to seek, find, preserve, and cherish their authentic, divine self. Free will also provides a person with the opportunity to review their choices and paths and to redirect themselves any time they feel out of alignment. Alignment is one of those circumstances when a person feels that the piece of the puzzle that they are trying to squeeze into their life just doesn't fit—in some way it's the wrong shape. The most powerful sign of misalignment is discomfort. It's important to check into the self and do an internal evaluation when we feel that something is "off." In any given circumstance an individual can change the situation or change their mind about it; one thing we always have control of is the way we think. The true power in life resides in our ability to think and choose freely.

In any loving, mature relationship or partnership, it is never the role of one individual to decide what another person should do or be at any given moment, regardless of how strongly or deeply a person loves the other. In fact, the more you love someone, the more you realize your supporting role is just to love and appreciate. I have found, through my years of living, that so many people attribute human characteristics to God. They truly believe that God is up in heaven, likely a male, making all the decisions and being responsible for every plight of person and mankind. For example, I've heard people say things like, "God gave me cancer, and I'm so thankful he took it away"; "Why does God make bad things happen to good people?"; "Why would God take that child away at such a young age?"; and "Why is God doing this to me?"

God or the consciousness of which I speak is not male or female. This energy has no characteristics of a human being. This loving energy is the greatest support we can have and the most loving energy or consciousness in which we can be immersed. God does not give people crosses to bear or foster suffering for some greater purpose. There is certainly a greater purpose to suffering, but it's not because God makes that decision or creates any conditions on this planet that would harm an individual or anything else. That's humanity at work, not God. Everything is always in perfect order, according to our co-created plan and our highest good—even when we cannot fathom that we would put obstacles in our path and support the challenges we face at a level of consciousness of which we have no awareness. The most perfect things in life will have had limited to zero access to humans. God does not create war or poverty or natural disasters or unnatural disasters. We have co-created our existence and the energy we exude. Our energy, along with the aggregate energies of the populace, are responsible for just about every aspect of our life. God just supplies the love and unwavering support in the form of divine light and energy that creates a consciousness that embraces each one of us in pure love—that same love from which we were created, hence made in the image of God. Female or male, all of this is completely irrelevant to God as we have lived many lifetimes as one or the other and we have experienced wonderful events and difficult hardships. When I refer to earth as the land of density, it is because none of us get away unscathed. Regardless of any particular position in life, we all have internal and external challenges. Earth has tough terrain to traverse, and I'm not talking landscape. We have stressors to overcome as soon as our feet hit the ground. There is so much beauty and abundance on earth, but there are also struggles and hardships and enough density for us to crawl out of every challenge a more evolved human. Light is love. The more light or love we carry within every cell of our being, the higher we vibrate. Spiritual evolution follows that escalation in vibration. There's no need to wonder how it will happen, it just will. A person will be led to awaken the knowledge and wisdom that already resides within. The perfect loving consciousness of **God is incapable of creating anything but love.**

We develop our co-created plan, in support with our multitude of divine guides within the consciousness of God. We are the authors of our lives, and we co-create these life plans with other souls that reincarnate with us so that we all help each other attain our objectives and goals. The elements of our plan allow for moment-to-moment decisions because earth is the free will planet, and that free will extends to the other side as well. So, as it turns out, it's not actually God's will . . . it's our will, or our combined wills if it is necessary for you to think that way. The only contribution God makes is supplying pure love and support in its finest form. Please allow me to repeat, God is devoid of any human characteristics or features. When we pray or ask for the intersession of any Ascended Master or Saint, our love extends into the ethers, and the energy of our love is accepted and combined with the light and love of these souls to provide additional love, courage, peace, strength, or whatever is needed to support the co-created plan of the person for whom you've requested the inter-session. In some way, perhaps unbeknown to us, all those prayers are answered. **Love and prayer hold an important and sacred place in life.** The Christ Consciousness is a way of life and death, and how we live affects how our afterlife will be as it is all related to the vibration of love. Our primary purpose in life is to love and be loved. The more love dictates our thoughts and actions, the higher our vibration of existence will be on the either side of the veil—earth or the other side.

Chapter Four

The Anatomy of Hope

The foundation of hope is love. Creating a successful outline, plan, or journey of hope is directly proportionate to our level and understanding of self-love, especially when our hopes need to be modified and the result of those changes have the potential for significant disappointment. It is from our love of self that every thought and action is derived. As everything we think, say, and do is a reflection from the inside out, so is the direction, slope, and elevation of our journey of hope. Love is the agent that directs our lives, even if we are totally unaware of how that system operates and we are not consciously developing a plan of hope.

There are two primary, fundamental emotions from which all other emotions and feelings are derived. They are love and fear. Every thought, emotion, and feeling is a result of these two facets. Love-based thoughts, feelings, and emotions feel good inside, and fear-based thoughts, feelings, and emotions don't. Some who frequently live in a state of fear, however, are immune to knowing the difference. They find comfort in their friend of fear because they know it so well. A goal is to understand which root system is providing nourishment to our development. **The root system that is fed the most will be allowed to flourish the most.**

Fear is an extremely noteworthy component and opponent when dissecting the anatomy of hope, because these two primary emotions or essences of thought—love and fear—provide the building blocks of life. This bifurcated root system is fundamental to the creation of our thoughts, and hence everything else. Physiologically, a gift we were bestowed in the creation of our physical bodies is the impossibility of having love and fear occupy our thoughts at the same time. This is called the "law of substitution." The basis of this principle is that two opposing thoughts cannot occur at the same time. An individual can vacillate between love and fear within milliseconds, but both love and fear cannot be present within our thoughts and feelings at the same time. Acknowledging this principle or gift allows a person to learn to identify the presence of fear and replace it with love, thereby freeing themselves to insert peace and joy where fear formerly festered. There are many faces of fear, as this root system maintains a hold on much of the clutter we work on within the shadows of our being. The many facets of fear decrease our vibration of love and can result in negative ramifications up to and including dis-ease. Anger, resentment, animosity, negative attitudes, pessimism, moodiness, addiction, and self-loathing are all examples of fear-based thoughts and feelings. Love-based thoughts and feelings, however, increase the vibration of our being and result in a life filled with greater joy and happiness. The latter is not a life without challenge or sadness or disappointment, but it is a life where those thoughts and emotions are temporary and don't rule our existence. Self-mastery and our ability to control fear does not mean that we can or will experience a life without fear. It means that we will have self-awareness and self-control to allow courage and resilience to recognize and overcome fear. Fear affects everyone. We are all afraid of something, but learning to control fear is paramount to living a life that is not paralyzed by fear or spent self-sabotaging ourselves with self-fulfilling prophesies. The principle of concentration is that whatever we focus on increases in size or intensity. That is why it's so important to be mindful of our thoughts and our fears and our obsessions. If an individual believes they can't, they can't. If a person believes they will fail, they will fail. If an individual recognizes that failure is a possibility but views failure as simply a redirection from what is in our ultimate best interest and just another opportunity to learn and grow, circumstances that one would accept as failure take on an entirely different meaning. Learning to accept that there is a multitude of redirections in life and that accepting them with a positive attitude makes all the difference in our level of happiness, joy, and confidence as we navigate the huge variations in life's terrain.

Hope comes naturally to most, and not many people stop to contemplate their level of hope or plan of hope in any given situation. Most of us just go along hoping that life will bring good health, joy, and abundance, and when the cards we are dealt at any given time dictate a deviation from that, our journey of hope adapts to the situation. Hope continues to be an important aspect of living because when we have hope or something to look forward to, the light at the end of the tunnel seems brighter—often regardless of how long we perceive the tunnel.

As mentioned previously, those who struggle to love themselves struggle to love others, and their view of life's challenges are often shaded with fear, anxiety, disappointment, resentment, and general discontent. Love must be the driver of our thoughts and actions. Love is the basis of hope whenever we think hopeful thoughts about ourselves and others. There are times when people who struggle with self-love feel hopeless. There is a frequency associated with the feeling of hopelessness, and since it's devoid of love, it's a dense—often dark—vibration. Sometimes people feel like death would be a better option. The only issue with death is that it may seem like a way out, but it's only another deeper way in, as it necessitates the growth and development on the other side instead of on earth.

As I said before, many people expect that when they die, every challenge, adversity, or internal struggle they have will disappear. That's not the case. Resolution of inside issues must continue for the soul to continue its love evolution, enriched vibration, and ascension into a higher level of consciousness. A person does not lose their fundamental personality characteristics when they die, nor do they lose their free will; free will is never taken away or lost. When souls arrive back home, however, **the will of the soul is never greater than the love of the Creator and Divinity,** and thus the soul understands the beauty of itself and others and becomes amenable to the will of our Creator energy or Source. It's another beginning that deepens the understanding that love is the ruler of all, and hence the inside work continues fervently. The environment back home is conducive to more love, not judgment. Judgment is a great separator on earth—it's one of the activities, either conscious or not, that provides a pull on people to believe they are separate from God and each other, thereby creating a dualistic approach to life—dualistic in that our Creator is up high in one place and we are all beneath the Creator, totally separate. This separateness then puts our Creator in a position to have all the authority above and below, thereby becoming the master puppeteer who pulls all the strings that subsequently create the necessity for rules and obedience. We are created from and by love, where the only judgment in life comes from the judgment of self. A human's life plan is in a state of continual co-creation where our Source provides love, support, and guidance.

On the other side, it is much easier to seek understanding of the self because of the saturation level of unconditional love, divine resources, and support. Healing can occur in any state of being, but there's incredible vibrational value to healing on earth because of the sludge, challenges, temptations, stress, and difficulty of earthly living. Although only love matters back home, healing is still a necessity for many, and it is not automatic upon reentry. Healing takes desire and effort. In this context, healing is the process of gaining self-mastery on all levels. On earth it is necessitated from the inside out—back home, there's only the inside to work on. Sometimes the healing includes working with the spirits of souls still in the flesh. Sounds crazy, but I'm talking about souls resolving issues by working with humans who are still alive on earth. Commonly, to resolve these kinds of issues, it becomes necessary to forgive and be forgiven. There is no judgment, except that which the soul judges about itself and its life choices.

Many have no idea that they have the choice to evolve on earth or back home, but the eventual evolution is pretty much nonnegotiable and always desired and never forced. Soul evolution always proceeds in one direction. For example, there is no such thing as a step backward on earth when it comes to enriching one's vibration of love. If a person thinks they healed or resolved some issue in their life and finds this issue creeping up again, it's not because they de-evolved and took a step back. The reason is because they evolved to a higher level of consciousness and became able to address deeper elements of the issue where additional healing was needed. Think of time as a spiral, not linear. Some souls are at it for lifetimes and lifetimes—hundreds or thousands of earth years. Thinking like a human, being stuck in dogma or allowing the ego to dominate often leads to a lack of awareness and slows the self-realization process.

Figuratively speaking, even the darkest souls, should they decide to open their hearts with a pinhole of light and love for themselves and Source, would subsequently allow the light of love to flood and penetrate those barriers. The light would shatter the shackles of their darkness in an instant. It would allow them to accelerate their vibration and consciousness closer to the Oneness of Source with just a sincere decision. Sometimes it's so hard for souls to forgive or shed their belief that they are totally separate from God and everyone. This can create an existence of darkness and isolation back home, but know that isolation is completely by choice of the individual and not by our Source. Some would refer to this as hell.

Hope defined as a noun is a feeling or expectation or a desire for a certain outcome. As a verb, it's wanting some outcome, hoping that we get what we desire for us or another being. We can create the conditions for a healthy life for ourselves, our children, our pets, and so on. We can ensure healthy eating, exercise, and prevention and early detection of disease, but we still can't control what's meant to be. Hope can be reasonable or realistic or just a wish that will never actually come to fruition. It's important to be honest with ourselves and others. As with wishes, when they are attainable and realistic, instead of wishing, it's essential to create the conditions for that wish to come true. We have so much more power than many think. This power doesn't come from money or status or a position of power or authority, but it comes from within, for we have the power to create the conditions of our lives by using our thoughts. This is not a new concept. It's called the principle of belief. This principle states that we create our reality by our thoughts as everything we see and experience originates as thought, thereby making the mind the most powerful tool because it creates our existence. In summary, this principle represents the truth that our reality is created by our perceptions and our minds. It's not a new concept; Buddha said, "What we think, we become." Jesus Christ said, "As ye think, so shall ye be." Marcus Aurelius said, "Our life is what our thoughts make it." Gandhi said, "Your beliefs become your thoughts, your thoughts become your words, your words become your actions, your actions become your habits, your habits become your values, and your values become your destiny."

Resilience is the cousin of hope because it's the ingredient in the recipe of life that gets you through the tough times. Resilience and hope have a linear relationship for as resilience rises through strength and the ability to cope with life's challenges, the journey of hope is consistently sustained throughout, even with its fluctuations in meaning and presentation. People who are resilient tend to accept that there's a reason for everything and that every challenge offers an opportunity for growth—whether it be physical, emotional, mental, or spiritual. These elements of being are so closely intertwined that they all depend on the other to create who we are at any given time in life. If you accept that there are no failures in life and just redirections, then you also accept that every relationship or experience had value and purpose at some level. Sometimes we can figure out the key metric(s) in that learning curve, and sometimes they will elude us for years or until we transition to the other side, as the full dataset of the existence of our soul can be accessed.

To successfully navigate the peaks and valleys of life,

we need to have a greater understanding of the life of a soul. We need to believe that we do not maintain the full dataset for our lives or the lives of anyone else. On earth, we often have an incredible lack of awareness of how and why the struggles of life are put in our path and by whom . . . and most of the time, most people would never believe these struggles are put there by themselves.

Chapter Five

The Universal Life Force, Religion & Accountability

To really understand how hope can enrich our resil-ience and keep us moving forward during a challenge, it's important we evaluate how we think about a multitude of issues and understand the triggers that upset us and how our mind processes information and solves problems. As with failures, mistakes are also redirections of one kind or another. It's also essential to keep an open mind and recognize that some of the beliefs or premises we have been taught and hold close to our hearts may be flawed or incomplete.

Religion is one of those subjects I usually avoid with people unless I think they're extremely open-minded. When people get to know me, they seem curious about my beliefs for some reason, and I get asked many ques-tions I've answered in the books I've written. My religion is love. It's the understanding that we are created from love and the threads of our being are woven together to create a tapestry of Oneness. This includes all of nature and all animals. We are all spiritual beings having a physical ex-perience, and when our souls return home to the vibration of Oneness, our spirits are united in love and familiarity. My religion is the practice of walking each day in the con-sciousness of love, kindness, tolerance, and forgiveness. Notice I said "is the practice"—as it's a never-ending journey of self-mastery, exercising those values to the best of my ability each day, understanding that it is in giving that we receive, it is by loving that we are loved, and every one of us is a work in progress.

I find there are some people who clutch onto their dogmatic religious beliefs and use that structure to bring order and understanding to their lives, and they don't want to venture out into any other spectrum of belief. That is great and I'm sure it makes life and challenges more defined and easier to accept. Other people may have a strong spirituality and love for all and accept only the parts of any specific religion that resonate with them. There are others who have a strong religious foundation or attachment but allow love to fuel their thoughts and actions, in accordance with the dogmatic beliefs they hold close to their heart. There are others who have no religious structure or affiliation, no book or prophet, but live their lives as love would, having a very deep connection to spirit and being a light to the world through kindness, respect, and gratitude. Since everything we say and do is a reflection from the inside out, an individual's level of kindness and positive thinking is affected by their belief systems in total. Everything is usually in perfect order, and all of us are functioning the best we can with what we have to work with within ourselves and our beliefs. I've noticed that extremely religious people, however, can be judgmental and hard on themselves—feeling unworthy of many of life's gifts or beating themselves up for not fitting the mold or doing something that was "against" their religion—divorce seems to be a common example. Every relationship has great value, and people sometimes marry to work out karmic issues between them but develop a co-created plan with the intention to divorce for whatever reasons rest within their highest good and the highest good of those children who choose to be offspring of the couple. There's a reason for everything. There have been numerous individuals over the years who have sought spiritual counseling from me because they were in a place where the religion of their youth created gaps in their reality, and they were searching for truth that resonated within them and didn't necessarily follow a prescribed recipe for salvation or what they were taught growing up. Whatever the situation, it haunted them and caused mental and emotional anguish or issues they could not let go because they struggled with the deeply engrained belief system they were taught. Some felt like they were drowning in guilt because internally they believed otherwise but externally they had to either keep quiet and fake it or be alienated by their families or friends. This indoctrination negatively affected their lives, and they sought relief from what they deeply knew could not be true but were the accepted teachings of their childhoods or the accepted truths of their families—often the pressure from families who don't truly understand the possibilities of each situation that can alienate children and loved ones unnecessarily. Truth can often be found from your experience, self-discovery, or from direct communication with the God within you. Regardless of any religious rules, guidelines, or dogmas within specific religious institutions, the truth is the truth. Sometimes we know what's true and other times we trust information coming from other sources; therefore, discernment is of great value, and this gift resides within our minds, hearts and spirits. Our spirit or higher self knows the truth that our soul searches to find, another one of humanity's purposes on earth, the free will planet in the cosmos.

Buddhism, Confucianism, Taoism, Sikhism. Christianity, Unitarianism, Native Spirituality, Zoroastrianism, Jainism, Judaism, Islam, Baha'i Faith, and Hinduism are organized religions that offer the world a home of faith. Some enter their faiths from birth, and others choose their religion because the primary beliefs resonate within them. Although there is great variation among these religions, love is the one common thread that weaves them all together. There is likely no dispute that love is the one given truth among all. Each religion has their own culture or traditions, but all have a recognition that we should treat others as we treat ourselves, that kindness is the way, and that we are all connected to each other in some fashion. Regardless of anyone's beliefs or lack thereof, it's vital to respect all religions and traditions and recognize that they play a vital role in our world.

One must remember that with all religions, however, not every element of the dogma is necessarily the truth or the only truth but represents the message or messages that were triumphant in the founders' quest to establish a particular dogma, help define behavior, or provide the potential for a better life to the people. Perhaps the founders were the most powerful or popular of their day, or perhaps they were the beliefs of the most influential political or religious leaders. Recognizing that each precious religion on this planet has a different dogma and sometimes very different beliefs, the variation often renders confusion related to the understanding or reconciliation of truth within the variation in beliefs.

For example, the concept that death shows favoritism to one form of religion over another is unrealistic and inconceivable. There are many jokes about Catholics thinking they will dominate the heavens, and all others will be relegated to lesser areas. Truth is truth and it transcends all religions. There are no secrets when it comes to truth; there is awareness and discernment. There is tradition and rules and there is faith and a spiritual knowing—it's imperative to know the difference. I'm sure there were many who had their hearts in the right place and really tried to help humanity find God through the wisdom they gathered millennia ago. It's likely that there were those who watched a world they thought may be falling apart and they tried desperately to convince people to live within certain guidelines to protect themselves from evil and damnation. Any control or manipulation may have been thought to be in the best interest of the populace, but manipulation in any form renders seen and unseen limitations and unintended consequences.

When I think about my own journey, I love that as a child I was raised Roman Catholic. In fact, much that I write about is more related to that religion than others because I have the most familiarity with it, and I was taught most of the tenets that established the Roman Catholic Church when I was young. It was like learning to walk before I could learn to run. It provided a foundation to build upon for when my level of spiritualism surpassed my beliefs in the dogma. It provided a credible framework for me as a child and convinced me that I was never alone and had protection around the clock—very helpful beliefs as I steered through the challenges of my youth. Regardless of church teaching, when I was young, Jesus was always my best friend, confidant, and protector. I leaned on him for everything—especially when my mother was not well and after she died. After her death, as often as I spoke to her and asked for her intercession, I knew Jesus had a skill set that transcended most, and he could help me even more than she could! God was somebody totally different, but I kept that a secret. Many religions accept Jesus as a

great prophet. Many understand that he is a true ascended master and teacher whose soul vibrates to the highest
level, in conjunction with the consciousness of God, but
Christianity is the only religion I mentioned that believes in
the mystery of the trinity whereby Jesus is God, or God's
only son. Perhaps I had cell memory from another lifetime
(substantiated with a past life regression when I was in my
forties where my soul lived at the time of Christ) or I wasn't
fully immersed in amnesia regarding our relationship, but
there was never a question, regardless of church teaching,
sermons, or anything else I listened to as a young girl, that
Jesus and God were the same energy. For me, the energies were always different, but the similarities and overlap
ran deep. It's kind of funny . . . back then he was my older
brother, but now we are the same age! I understand it's the
fundamental tenet of the Catholic religion, and it's one of
the dogmatic mysteries, but I know existence on the other
side is not what is taught on earth. He lived the way of
love, peace, kindness, and forgiveness—truly characteristics for all of us to emulate. Jesus was immersed within the
Christ Consciousness, and this showed in all his words and
deeds, and he remains one of the most loved and revered
ascended masters on the other side, but none are put
on a pedestal or have a special cutout. His soul is among
the most highly evolved that exist, but his is among other
highly evolved beings of light, many of whom directed
the development of other organized religions or philosophies or achieved that level of enlightenment through
a life devoted to love. Having said that, his soul, like all
others, has the ability to be ubiquitous—being in many
places at one time or multi-locate. The position of avatar,
ascended master, or prophet is a position that is available
to all who seek and attain that high level of vibration of
love and enlightenment. Jesus's life and teachings were

beyond profound as he was one of the most incredibly gifted and connected souls to incarnate the earth. He was a clairaudient and clairsentient mystic who caused apocalyptic changes to the world he found. He altered the world in any and every way he could. He did not deal with all the issues that were abhorrent in his day, such as slavery or the inequality of people, as I'd guess his earthy purpose was significant and time-consuming enough without including all that—we all decide what battles to pick. Like any evolved spiritualist, his plan included the teaching of the message that would awaken the people to love and understanding of the absence of death. His message of love, acceptance, and tolerance underscored his every word and deed. Too often Jesus's true messages have been lost. He would not support rules, regulations, and guidelines of any organized religion that alienate many of the individuals who need love and understanding the most. He exemplified his philosophies by hanging out with all the people who were rejected by society, and even some of his disciples had suspicious pasts. Regardless of what the dogma taught me, I knew him . . . I felt him . . . I communicated with him . . . I loved him, and he was and still is a best friend and precious confidant.

God was a totally different entity to me. Being young and not understanding consciousness or energy, my perception was that God was a nice, yet strict, all-knowing man with white hair and a beard who sat on a throne in heaven—which was located way up high in the sky. He made all the decisions and called all the shots. Today I obviously believe in a much different God as our Source is a vibration of love—an energy or consciousness that is all knowing and all loving and has **zero** characteristics of humanity. In true love, there is no power struggle or manipulation. It makes no sense that an all-loving consciousness picks and chooses anything for anyone. It is also impossible for an energy of pure love to create anything but love. It still is a mystery for the human mind to comprehend, but it is understandable if you accept some basic principles of love, vibration, and existence. It's an inside job to see what concepts resonate as truth and inquire within to answer these questions. Remember, heaven is not a place, it's a vibration, and every individual has formulated a life plan for their highest good toward the evolution and ascension of their soul. Truly, we die as we have lived and return to a process of ascension propelled by love, wisdom, and the spiritual evolution and growth of the soul.

I will always remember my First Holy Communion, all dressed in white with a beautiful dress, veil, new shoes, and lovely white purse with a beautiful prayer book and rosary beads that I still cherish. What an honor it was to finally be old and smart enough (seven years old) to share in the meal of the Mass. It was all so simple then. Unaware that the stories were allegorical, words in the Bible were accepted at face value and differences were ignored. Around that same age of seven, I recall Santa, the Easter Bunny, and the Tooth Fairy being voted off the island, but thankfully the people didn't lie about God—the world around me just seemed to make him think and judge as a human. God, like Santa, knew everything about me and everything I was doing, but unlike Santa, who didn't really exist, God controlled all worldly and personal afflictions and events. I could never understand how God could love us and make bad things happen. My mother and father would never let anything happen to me because they loved me, and supposedly God loved me more. At that time, my mother's answer would have been, "There is a reason for everything, and we should just trust God." I totally agree with that, but now I understand the work of human hands and the level of influence we have on our own lives and our individual and aggregate life plans, and actually so does she—we have both evolved in the over fifty years she's resided on the other side. In fact, a great deal of my spiritual education and inspiration has been provided by her. In my late thirties and early forties, I was drawn to explore simplistic quantum physics, different religious beliefs, spiritualism, the Gnostics, aspects of the Roman Empire, and the historical Jesus and facets of the Bible of antiquity versus the Bible of today (such as reincarnation, lost Gospels, heretical parchments, and added stories). I received my Doctor of Divinity from the American Institute of Holistic Theology when I was fifty years old. Those were my years of self-discovery as well as expanding my exposure to elements of spirituality that eluded me. I was forty-three when I became the CEO of the largest, most comprehensive physician-owned cancer center in Central New York. My self-mastery journey catapulted in my forties and early fifties as I dove headfirst into my own self-mastery journey, sharing whatever I could along the way with my family, friends, and colleagues—actually anyone who was interested or would listen! It became clear to me that every relationship we have depends upon the relationship we have with ourselves. I knew if people could see the best in themselves and foster their own self-mastery journey, with good communication, clear expectations, and a dedication to the good of the whole, the desire to provide outstanding patient care would become the objective of each employee, and the success from our combined energies would have no limits. These concepts precipitated my first two books, *Building the Team from the Inside-Out* and *A Human's Purpose by Millie the Dog*.

Many souls have evolved in consciousness to reap higher levels of knowledge and wisdom that they have developed through lifetimes. This opportunity is available to every soul. Thousands of years ago, information was shared verbally. The first Gospel of Mark was written about seventy years after the death of Jesus. The rest of the Canonical Gospels, Matthew, Luke, and John, are estimated to have been completed around one hundred years after the death of Jesus. I imagine that is one of the reasons why information within the Gospels differs so much. There are many variations among them. Many people have received their information about the birth, life, and death of Jesus from Hollywood and have never actually read and compared the Gospels.

The first meeting to establish consensus of the Roman Catholic Church was called by Constantine in 325 CE. He requested the presence of over one thousand bishops to gather and discuss aspects of the Roman Catholic faith to gain standardization in the dogma. This meeting was called the first Council of Nicaea. One of the most critical objectives of the meeting was to have these humans finalize Jesus's relationship to God. The bishops concluded and consensus set the path for the future when the decision was made that Jesus is the only Son of God. The Nicene Creed was created at this time to eliminate any confusion regarding the most important tenets of the Roman Catholic religion and provide a proclamation of faith for centuries to come. An excerpt from the Nicene Creed is as follows, "I believe in one Lord, Jesus Christ, the only Son of God, eternally begotten by the Father, God from God, Light from Light, true God from true God."

It was likely that the stories of Jesus's virgin birth, miracles including the raising of the dead, and his death and resurrection played an important part in their decision-making. For me, however, their decisions underscore the separation between God, Jesus, and everyone else. It doesn't really foster us to look to the God within and know that we are all one. It's interesting that there are other individuals who were said to be born of a virgin birth and perform miracles, including raising the dead. It is taught that Krishna, the Hindu god, was born of a holy virgin. In fact, both Krishna and Jesus are held to be God incarnate by their two respective religions. In a case like this, which religion is correct? I'm sure there is as much passion and belief within both religions, and each follower's beliefs are steadfast.

When I was studying religion from a historical perspective, I was drawn to several lecture series by Professor Bart Ehrman. He is a well-known professor of religion at University of North Carolina at Chapel Hill. He has several outstanding lecture series from the Teaching Company, now known as The Great Courses. Professor Ehrman is an author and a well-known agnostic atheist. I've read that in the past, Professor Ehrman started his classes by introducing the following story as a description of a famous man from the ancient world:

> Before he was born, his mother had a visitor from heaven who told her that her son would not be a mere mortal, but in fact would be divine. His birth was accompanied by unusual divine signs in heaven. As an adult, he left his home to engage in an itinerant preaching ministry. He gathered a number of followers around him who became convinced that he was no ordinary human, but that he was the Son of God, and he did miracles to confirm them in their beliefs. He could heal the sick, cast out demons, and raise the dead. At the end of his life, he aroused opposition among the ruling authorities of Rome and was put on trial. But they could not kill

is soul. He ascended to heaven and continues to live there until this day. To prove that he lived on after leaving his earthly orb, he appeared again to at least one of his doubting followers, who became convinced that in fact, he remains with us even now. Later, some of his followers wrote books about him, and we can still read about him today.

Perhaps you are thinking that he is referring to Jesus Christ, and you may be thinking that many of the students identified the famous man as such too. You may be surprised that Professor Ehrman was not speaking of Jesus, but he was referring to Apollonius of Tyana. Apollonius was an ancient Greek philosopher from the Roman province of Cappadocia. It's reported he lived from around 3 BCE to about 97 CE. I've read that many believed he was divine and could save humanity. He was a spiritual teacher who likely changed his world by sharing a message of love. He is known to have established egalitarian communities among his followers that became known as the Essenes. I have read accounts of Jesus spending a great deal of time studying and learning as an Essene and spending time in many places in the Mediterranean world and India in his young adulthood before he returned to Jerusalem prior to his death. It's reported that Apollonius was a charismatic teacher and miracle worker, and many temples were built in his honor all over the Mediterranean world, through Mesopotamia and into India. I've also read that the mathematician Pythagoras was heavily influenced by Apollonius's philosophies.

I'm not trying to convince you to abandon your religious beliefs and change your mind about who Jesus is or isn't or what heaven or the other side is or isn't. I'm trying to offer information that underscores that regardless of how big your sphere of knowledge and knowing are, there is always truth and facts that rest outside your circle of knowledge. There is much we don't know and much we are taught that is accepted without question or self-study that has been influenced by humans for millennia. So, it's best to seek guidance from the love of the Creator that resides within each of us. Keep it simple, as the role and responsibility of love is just that: simple.

There were many in Jesus's day and thereafter who held him in their hearts and knew that special friendship. He helped them to understand that all things were made of love, and he wanted them to carry his message of pure love, light, hope, and gratitude. Living this message of love is one of a human's purposes of incarnating on earth. There's no need to wear this on your sleeve or talk or boast about it. There is no mandate to attend religious services, recite special prayers or be a member of any organized religious affiliation. The only mandate is to love yourself, which then allows you to love others; to see the goodness and perfection within the self, thereby having the ability to see the goodness in others and become tolerant, especially when philosophies and beliefs differ; to understand that regardless of how smart or knowledgeable you are, there is much you and I are totally clueless about.

The purpose of being is to BE LOVE. Be love with every breath and every thought, and that means making sure everyone takes good care of themselves so they can be of assistance to others. It means always doing the right thing, being kind, fulfilling your vocations, and making the world a better place in accordance with the greatest good of the whole. It's also important to take time out to rest. It's essential to take time for ourselves to contemplate life and feel love. That can happen in a place of worship, a bathtub, on a hill, out on a run, in a lounge chair in the yard, and on and on. There are numerous activities that can nicely put your sacred heart and your mind at rest. The objective is to take time to be—just be.

I was educated in public schools until high school when I attended an all-girls Catholic high school that merged with an all-boys Catholic high school when I was a senior. I loved the nuns and priests who taught us. They were loving and kind. Some were good teachers, and others were just teaching. There was a beautiful level of respect and reverence for those who dedicated their lives to God back then—those who gave up having sex and a family and left home to serve others wherever they were assigned. I was fortunate to never have any kind of abuse issue on which millions of dollars have been spent to offer some level of mitigation. I am fortunate that I have never known a nun who didn't have her heart in the right place, and there has never been one I have not genuinely loved. If they were gay or in love with priests, it never mattered to me, and it was none of anyone's business anyway. Like many, they upheld the most important aspects of their man-made oath of love and service to others. We know being single was not a prerequisite to be a disciple of Jesus as many were married. We also know he had many female followers. His most knowledgeable, loved, and evolved disciple was actually a woman, Marium of Migdal, also known as Mary Magdalene. She came to earth with a great purpose and is known as the Avatar of the Divine Feminine Christ Consciousness. She and Yeshua, or Jesus, were immersed within the Christ Consciousness and worked in tandem to teach the way of love, compassion, peace, and joy. You may be surprised to know her Gospel exists today. It is obviously a noncanonical text (not in the Bible). It was discovered in 1896 in a fifth-century papyrus codex written in Coptic. The Gospel of Mary Magdalene underscores that she was a spiritual teacher. Her wisdom and enlightenment encourage us to look within for the answers we seek. After Jesus's death, Mary relocated to France where she helped to create a network of communities called the *Cathars* or "pure ones." The Cathars were wiped out by the Catholic Church under the direction of Pope Innocent III in the Albigensian Crusade in the thirteenth century (1209–1229), when the church was on a mission to further eliminate any heretical documents or ministries. From my extremely limited research, there appears to be conflicting documentation related to the beliefs of the Cathars, which is not unusual for something that existed centuries ago and no longer exists. What I do know is that Mary Magdalene is very active today within our world, as is Jesus and his mother Mary. Together, they work to balance the masculine and feminine energies for love, peace, and harmony. There are many who can genuinely channel Mary Magdalene, and we've learned a lot about Jesus and their teachings from her communications. Even today, they continue to teach *the way.*

In the Gospel of Mary Magdalene, Jesus said to his disciples, "'Go then and preach the gospel about the kingdom. Don't lay down any rules beyond what I've given you, nor make a law like the lawgiver, lest you be bound by it.' When he said these things, he left."

In the book by Noah Press, *The Gospel of Mary Magdalene: Exploring Divine Spiritual Wisdom*, he adds excellent commentary regarding the interpretation of this noncanonical gospel. His commentary on the aforementioned statement is as follows:

If the disciples set up new rules and laws, they are likely to restrict themselves as well. Rules and laws can be a hindrance to those who are attempting to live out their spiritual nature. They work against the freedom and insight that accomplishes salvation. Jesus taught us what is essential to salvation, and nothing should be added to it. For them, following Jesus didn't mean observing rules but living in a particular way, in love, truth and freedom. Jesus showed us how to do this—in what he taught, how he loved and his acting out of patience, love and forgiveness. Jesus' teachings, then are not legalistic. The disciples are to go out and teach others, he says, but they are not to add rules or laws of their own devising, which are more likely to hinder than enlighten them.

This Gospel of Mary Magdalene was one of a group of writings found at different archaeological sites and at different times by different people throughout history. Among others, at the time of their use, they were buried for safe keeping, as all noncanonical works were considered heretical and were mandated to be destroyed. To ignore information found in these works just upholds the original dictum of censorship. Many of the documents found are those associated with a type of religion or philosophy called Gnosticism. Gnostics were abundant between the first and third centuries after Christ. *Gnosis* means "knowing," and Gnostics believed it was not the law that mattered but the spirit.

The disciples knew of Jesus's love for Mary Magdalene. They knew that Jesus shared information with her that they did not share with them, and it's documented in Gnostic texts that it made the disciples angry. As always, only those with ears to hear can hear, and Jesus shared things with Mary because she was spiritually evolved and enlightened. In the Gospel of Mary Magdalene, after Jesus's death, the disciples asked Mary to share some of the things that Jesus shared with her that they didn't know. Here are a few excerpts from the Gospel of Mary Magdalene after she shared some of the private teachings between her and Jesus:

> In response Andrew said [to] the brothers, "Say what you will about what she's said, I myself don't believe that the Savior said these things, because these teachings seem like different ideas." In response Peter spoke out with the same concerns. He asked them concerning the Savior: "He didn't speak with a woman without our knowledge and not publicly with us, did he? Did he prefer her to us?" Then Mary wept and said to Peter, "My brother Peter, what are you thinking? Do you really think that I thought this up by myself in my heart, or that I'm lying about the Savior?" In response Levi said to Peter, "Peter, you've always been angry. Now I see you debating with this woman like the adversaries. But if the Savior made her worthy, who are you then to reject her? Surely the Savior knows her very well. That's why he loved her more than us. Rather, we should be ashamed, clothe ourselves with perfect Humanity, acquire it for ourselves as he instructed us, and preach the gospel, not laying down any other rule or other law beyond what the Savior said."

As the Roman Catholic Church was created, not only did they ignore and attempt to destroy information that differed from what they wanted to last in perpetuity, they also would not and could not accept wisdom coming from Mary Magdalene, primarily because she was a woman and that was totally unacceptable at that time. It's also important to mention that Mary was never a prostitute. I read that when the Bible of antiquity is compared to the Bible used today, the phrase, "Let he who is without sin cast the first stone," was not written. I will admit, it's a heck of a great sentence with incredible practical meaning, but what I'm trying to convey is that we don't know what we don't know. You don't know what you don't know. In addition, none of us, in the physical form we inhabit today, were present at the time of Christ, and stories and memories were shared person to person for many, many years before the canonical Gospels were written. Play the telephone game where one person tells a story to another and allow them to tell at least nine others. Pay attention to the tenth person's recollection of the story and see if and how it differs. We used to play this game in kindergarten, and I had my staff play it at a staff meeting many years ago. The take-home message is that when something is shared only verbally, it usually takes on the interpretation or embellishment of the narrator with added or deleted details because that's how humans process information.

Also, in the Gospel of Mary Magdalene, it is written, "When the Blessed One said these things, he greeted them all and said, 'Peace be with you! Acquire my peace. Be careful not to let anyone mislead you by saying, "Look over here! Or look over there!" Because the Son of Humanity exists within you. Follow him! Those who seek him will find him.'"

Jesus taught that we cannot receive peace or internal harmony and balance passively. This is an inside job that does not and cannot depend on another person or a favorable outcome that we seek. When we recall the true message of the Christ, that of love and forgiveness, of sincerity and kindness, of helpfulness and support for ourselves and others, we can find peace. As this peace expands, our world will become a better place.

We continue to live in a patriarchal society of structure, which includes the Roman Catholic Church. They maintain a narrow view on priests, and perhaps that has led to some of the power and abuse issues the church has experienced. Those of the clergy who have abused children should not be excused, and knowing that so many convicted priests and bishops were revered at one time underscores the confusion and post-traumatic stress that so many people experience. I remember when the list of child sex offenders who were priests and bishops was distributed; it was so extensive I found it rather unfathomable. Thinking of how these men were adored and respected by their congregations underscored how misleading the whole ministry can be because of the *influence of ordinary people with the same dysfunctions as nonreligious vocations.* Thinking of how often they listened to confessions and gave advice and penance, while they broke not only the law but their priestly vows, is unconscionable.

In July of 2007, one of my dearest friends and high school biology teacher, who had been a nun for most of her life and left her community after decades of sacrifice, sent me a copy of an article from the *Associated Press*, from Lorenzago Di Cadore, Italy, that was entitled, "Pope Reasserts other Christian groups not true churches." It starts, "Pope Benedict XVI reasserted the primacy of the Roman Catholic Church, approving a document released Tuesday that says other Christian communities are either **defective** or not true churches and Catholicism provides the only true path to salvation" (emphasis mine).

She was livid when she read this article, and her note that accompanied it underscored the continual disappointments of the bureaucracy that catalyzed her leaving her community of sisters of charity. Statements like this underscore why so many are frustrated by elements of the Catholic Church and turned off by organized religion. The dogma really points to a desire by those who established the religion to control the masses and foster separation between an individual and the hierarchy of the church and God. One such example is the doctrine of infallibility. This doctrine hinges on the Catholic dogma of papal supremacy whereby the authority of the pope governs what is and what is not accepted as formal beliefs in the Catholic Church. I think the last thing Jesus would call the faithful of a different religion is **defective.** What is defective is the delusion of the church regarding their rules, regulations, and the absence of the true message of the Christ in many instances. Throughout the history of the Roman Catholic Church, there have been many popes, some of whom have emulated the Christ Consciousness and others who have deviated far from that path. Of recent, Pope Francis (1936–2025) was a pope of the people who truly exemplified the consciousness of the Christ, having put love first in all instances. One of his quotes that I think explains the person and pope he represented is, "What is the most important subject to learn in life? To learn love."

I was very upset when my Reiki practice for cancer patients began to exclude devout Catholics because they were told it was against their religion. On March 25, 2009, a document called, "Guidelines for Evaluating Reiki as an Alternative Therapy" was released by a Committee on Doctrine from the United States Conference of Catholic Bishops. It was fully executed by eight bishops from various communities around the country. In summary, they cited that Reiki therapy is not compatible with either Christian teaching or scientific evidence, and they advised it would be inappropriate for any Catholic institution such as healthcare facilities, retreat centers, and so on to promote or provide Reiki therapy. It begins with, "The Church recognizing healing by divine grace and healing that utilizes the power of nature; however, Reiki is not included in such definitions." How ignorant these bishops were on this energy practice and the science of energy and vibrational healing. It includes statements such as, "Neither the Scriptures nor the Christian tradition as a whole speak of the natural world based on 'universal life energy.'" The document advises of important dangers such as superstition that will corrupt one's worship of God. The document states that "universal life energy" is unknown to natural science. It states, "As the presence of such energy has not been observed by means of natural science, the justification for these therapies necessarily must come from something other than science." In their conclusion they state, "Reiki therapy finds no support either in the findings of natural science or in Christian belief. For a Catholic to believe in Reiki therapy presents insoluble problems." It continues, "Without justification either from Christian faith or natural science, a Catholic who puts his or her trust in Reiki would be operating in the realm of superstition, the no-man's-land that is neither faith nor science." As it turns out, only **one** of these bishops is on the list for documented and legally convicted sexual abuse. Years ago, when I first searched the names, the first two out of three were on the list, but when I searched to ensure I was correct for the writing of this book, only one name remained. I shall assume the allegations were not upheld for the other. In any event, I ask, on what *man's-land* is what the priests and bishops who have been convicted or who have supported or covered up this conduct, such as child sex abuse, acceptable? It's also hard to ignore the millions of dollars spent to defend these offenders or provide settlements to the victims. The money for these settlements has not come from Rome and the top of the Catholic Church hierarchy. The money has come from parishioners from yesterday, today, and tomorrow.

There have been many times in history that people have been guided by the misguided, and fear and control have been the motivating and underlying factors in such activity. In the 1500s, the church was adamant that the sun revolved around the earth because God made it that way. Church and political leaders would not accept the scientific theory to the contrary that the earth orbited around the sun. That fact, if true, would have negated some of the religious beliefs at that time. It must have been too difficult to explain, accept, or update the dogma, so instead they fought hard to hold on to their position. Copernicus was at odds with the church because of the development of his heliocentric theory, a hypothesis that disputed the widely accepted belief that the earth was the center of the universe. Galileo was deemed a heretic and was imprisoned and tried by the Inquisition after his book was published that hypothesized that the earth and the other planets revolved around the sun and not the other way around. Galileo put his life at risk to convince the religious establishment that the Copernican model of the solar system, in which the earth and other planets revolved around the sun represented reality. That was not the first or last time the church almost sacrificed or sacrificed a human life because an individual would not agree to uphold the dogma of the day and compromise their integrity by lying about what they knew to be true. There were many times in history when death was the ramification for being a new voice of truth or the face of differing paradigms. Just read about the Inquisition, and you'll learn details you may not be aware of today.

Reiki is one of the most beautiful, spiritual, and sacred

energy practices that exists. It helps millions of people cope with a variety of issues each year. The actual modality does have elements specific to the healing art that was created by Mikao Usui in the late 1800s; however, he did not make up the concept of the universal life force that is available to everyone to utilize in the healing of themselves. The Reiki practitioner is merely a conduit for such energy balancing, and energy balancing can occur without formal Reiki training when someone understands the chakra and meridian systems of the human body. Vibrational or energy healing is taught and practiced by many by utilizing the human energy field.

The first human energy field to be well documented was the "field of the heart." In 1924, a man named Einthoven received the Nobel Prize for his accomplishments in energy research that lead to the electrocardiogram. Examples of medical technologies that utilize energy as healing or diagnostic modalities include but are not limited to medical imaging such as X-rays, MRIs, CT and PET scans; electrocardiograms, electroencephalograms, and electroretinograms; radiation therapy, CyberKnife, and proton beams; transcutaneous nerve stimulators; cardiac pacemakers and defibrillators; and lasers and electrocautery. Each modality uses energy to work, yet that energy is not visible to the naked eye.

The research of Einthoven and Berger (Berger studied electric fields of the brain resulting in the medical field of electroencephalography) established that organs such as the heart and brain produce bioelectric fields that travel through the tissues of the body and can be recorded with electrodes on the body surface, or even at distances that extend outside the body. Ampère's Law is a fundamental law in physics that says when currents flow through conductors such as wires or living tissues, magnetic fields

must be produced in the surrounding space. This provides a fundamental parameter for energy healing. If you need proof of our electromagnetic fields, go online and purchase energy balls. These are Ping-Pong-size balls with two small metal strips on each side. When the circuit is complete, the ball lights up and makes a buzzing noise. You can get a group of people in a circle. Have one hold onto the ball and touch one of the metal strips. Allow each person to touch the other person to complete the circuit and touch the other metal strip to wake up the ball. It's fun to do, as when one person breaks the circuit, the ball no longer lights up and the buzzing stops. I used these energy balls in my Reiki I classes so my students would truly understand that we are beings with electric currents flowing through our bodies. It is a fun and fascinating way to demonstrate the principles of electricity and conductivity.

Perhaps you recall as a child learning how clock makers realized that given a short amount of time, the pendulums of all the clocks in a room started to move back and forth at the same rate and direction as each other. This is attributable to the scientific principle of entrainment. It's the same explanation for why women who live together often have their periods at the same time. The history of entrainment is linked to a Dutch scientist named Christian Huygens in 1665. While working on the design of the pendulum clock, Huygens found that when he placed two of them on a wall near each other and swung the pendulums at different rates, they would eventually end up swinging in at the same rate. This is due to their mutual influence on one another. This is the phenomenon in physics called resonance, which was first observed in the seventeenth century. Entrainment is defined as the tendency for two oscillating bodies to lock into phase so that they vibrate in harmony. The principle of entrainment is universal, appearing in chemistry, pharmacology, biology, medicine, psychology, sociology, astronomy, architecture, and more. Another classic example is with individual pulsing heart muscle cells. When they are brought close together, they begin pulsing in synchrony. Entrainment is very evident in music, and many people purchase music with frequencies that aid in relaxation or sleep. Music can alter a mood, elicit a memory, and prompt emotional and mental changes.

In energy work, the practitioner learns how to relax and open or balance the client's energy centers called chakras. In doing this, their energy fields, through entrainment, develop similar frequencies that oscillate in harmony. The following illustrations attempt to explain what I'm referring to. In the first example, the two lines representing the energy field of the practitioner and client are out of sync and with time, in the second illustration they oscillate in harmony.

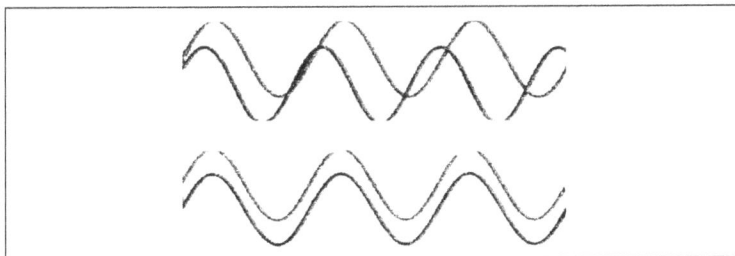

These harmonic frequencies that are developed within the bioelectric fields are measurable. Studies by Dr. Justa Smith using enzymes and magnetic fields also lend supportive scientific data to the presence of energy fields. Through the study of laboratory-induced, high-intensity magnetic fields, it has been proven that these fields can accelerate enzyme reaction rates. Dr. Smith used spectrophotometric methods to measure changes in enzyme activity and further demonstrated that energy healers can accelerate the kinetic activity of enzymes in a fashion similar to the effects of high-intensity magnetic fields. The experimental evidence suggests that energies of healers appear to be magnetic in nature; however, the biomagnetic fields of healers demonstrated properties that are entirely different from what is known about conventional magnetic fields.

Bernard Grad experimented with the effects of laying-on-of-hands healing on living systems. He discovered that the growth rate of plants could be accelerated by magnet-treated water as well as healer-treated water. Research chemist Robert Miller found that copper sulfate dissolved in regular distilled water formed jade-green crystals when it precipitated out of solution. If the copper sulfate was exposed to energies of healer's hands or a strong magnetic field, it always formed courser grained, turquoise-blue crystals. This phenomenon is likely the result of altered hydrogen bonding and changes in the chemical complexes. It was demonstrated that both healer's hands and magnets could accelerate the growth rates of plants, cause blue crystallization of copper sulfate, and increase enzyme reaction rates. Dr. John Zimmerman from the University of Colorado School of Medicine has added further evidence to suggest the magnetic nature of healing energy using SQUID (superconducting quantum interference device). He proved significant increases in the intensity of the magnetic fields emitted by healer's hands—several hundred times larger than background noise—yet far weaker than the levels required to produce enzyme effects in the lab. A quote by Dr. Richard Gerber provides a nice conclusion: "The direction of change in enzyme activity always seemed to mirror the natural cellular intelligence. The magnetic fields associated with healers are exceedingly weak, yet they have powerful biological and chemical effects."

C. W. Smith, the author of *Biological Effects of Weak Electromagnetic Fields* (pp. 81–107), includes the following summaries: the heart has the strongest biomagnetic field and has been measured to a distance of fifteen feet; the brain and all the organs of the body have their own biomagnetic fields surrounding them, and the fields pulsate at various frequencies and interact with each other; an organ will have a specific frequency when it's healthy and will move away from this frequency when it's not; the sum of the magnetic fields form a large aggregate biomagnetic field that surrounds the body—similar to what is called the "aura"; and the field interacts with other fields near the body, including the fields of other people.

I'm sure you can agree that the biomagnetic field of one person influences the biomagnetic field of another person. Have you ever felt a person enter a room before you've seen them? Have you ever thought, *My, you can cut the tension in this room with a knife?* Have you ever looked at a person and felt their bad mood? Now you can scientifically explain how you know these things. As science progresses and human minds reach outside their comfort zones, we see science explaining the unexplainable more and more every day.

Medical research demonstrates that devices producing pulsing magnetic fields of particular frequency can stimulate the healing of a variety of tissues. There is equipment used by many people, especially athletes, that takes advantage of the effects of pulsating electromagnetic field devices. Studies show these pulsating frequencies can improve muscle performance and improve blood circulation. I know it may be difficult to comprehend, but therapists from various schools of energy medicine can project, from their hands, fields with similar frequencies and intensities. Medical research and hands-on therapies are confirming each other, and the common denominator is the pulsating magnetic field, which is called a "biomagnetic field" when it emanates from the hands of a therapist.

It's silly to think that Catholics have the monopoly on the laying of hands and healing or any other self-pre-scribed truth. It makes no sense that only certain or special people can assist others to heal themselves through energy work. I studied Reiki for four years before becoming a Reiki master/teacher. I can tell you that the foundation of that healing is love and light. I can tell you that it has helped millions of people around the globe. I can tell you that for ten years, when I had the energy to get home from work at eight o'clock, I served clients who were cancer patients after my CEO hours, two days per week. I witnessed profound healing of the mind, body, and spirit. I can attest to the enrichment of my own faith and connection to God and all that is divine. I can also tell you that the more I began to understand about myself and the world, the less Catholic I became and the more spiritual I grew. I think this is the real fear within dogmas that don't support energy healing. You see, the earth and other planets of our solar system really do revolve around the sun—we are not the center of the universe. It's very true that practitioners and clients of energy healing have experiences of healing on many levels such that their personal relationship with their Creator and with the universal life energy becomes so enriched, the intermediary of the church becomes less essential. Perhaps that was the genuine, unspoken fear that motivated the lack of support for Reiki. The bishops who provided their summary about the dangers of Reiki must not have done their homework; however, they thought it acceptable to pontificate statements of a scientific nature that have no basis and are untrue.

I recall what one of my clients who was receiving radiation and chemotherapy weekly told me before one of her Reiki sessions. She expressed how she couldn't see the radiation beam, but she knew it was working because her tumors were shrinking. She also told me that she didn't know what I was doing during a Reiki treatment, as she couldn't see anything, but not only did she feel lighter and less tired and stressed when she left her treatment, her nausea and diarrhea post energy work would be gone for five days after a Reiki treatment. I saw her weekly for symptom management until her death. There are so many other beautiful stories I have from my Reiki practice. Another of my clients came to me after eleven consecutive brain metastases from lung cancer. One of our physicians thought perhaps Reiki could assist with the swelling of her brain as he told me he was out of treatment options. I provided Reiki treatments to her every week for several years. In addition to energy work, we talked. We talked about her life—the aspects that made her happy, disappointed, angry, and so on. She shocked the medical community by living ten years after we started her Reiki treatments. She remained cancer free for close to nine years after our first Reiki treatment as additional brain metastases ceased to develop during Reiki treatments. Was it a coincidence that she would have eleven brain metastases in a row and that they suddenly stopped when Reiki treatments started? She attributed this dramatic cease in cancerous brain lesions to Reiki and our spiritual work, as she became very spiritual during the time we were together, and she really looked within to heal many wounds of her past. I grew to love her very deeply, and I still feel her presence. I provided Reiki treatments to another client getting radiation treatments for a glioblastoma—cancer of the brain. I could feel the accumulation of radiation energy after each treatment. The energy from her last treatment was extremely palpable, and my hands never felt such a concentration of chaotic energy. My hands were on fire, and my hand chakras had never responded to that level of energetic chaos prior to this treatment. She would tell me after each treatment how less confused and more peaceful she felt—like her head calmed down. After her last session, she said the before and after was mind blowing. She lived for ten more years—which is remarkable for a person with a glioblastoma! I will always attribute part of her healing and longevity to our energy work that was provided in addition to conventional therapies.

The blessings that I witnessed when I provided Reiki therapy are available to anyone who puts forth the love, humility, and time to continue their self-mastery journey and become an energy practitioner. The more a person is engaged in energy work the more perceptive and intuitive they become. The path to being an excellent practitioner resides in the clearing of clutter within to be the best and brightest channel or conduit to the divine light and energy to assist the client to heal themselves. You should know that when I learned Reiki in 2002, I was skeptical. I was in my early forties, and I was not dissimilar to many and sought some kind of proof to solidify my path as an energy worker. I have always been a scientist at heart, searching for science to substantiate the wisdom passed down from thousands of years ago. It was around 2002 that cancer patients around the country, especially at large centers, were becoming more engaged in these healing modalities. After my research, a unique opportunity developed to establish an integrative therapy program and wellness center for our cancer patients and the community. That program is in its twenty-fourth year and remains supported by the physicians, leadership, and patients of the medical practice. I spent about four years preparing for my

Reiki master/teacher certification. The last year was spent volunteering to provide a minimum of one hundred hours to gain the experience and skill necessary to truly understand energy work and the nuances of communication between the client's body and spirit and the practitioner. I became dear friends with the individual who lovingly allowed me to perform the entire one hundred hours with her. She had limited knowledge of Reiki when we started, but like most cancer patients with a terminal diagnosis, she was very open to this work. She was diagnosed with metastatic breast cancer when she was in her thirties. When I provided the first treatment, I did it outside on my deck using an exercise mat because I hadn't even purchased a table yet. It was cloudy and thunderstorms were forecasted. I decided to work with the universe and asked mother earth to take that energy of the approaching thunderstorm and combine it with our energies for healing of her hip and femur, which she told me the orthopedic physician told her was hanging on by a thread. I even used a tuning fork that vibrates to a frequency that is beneficial for bone growth. When we were finished, I carried the exercise mat into my kitchen, and before I could close the door, it began to pour with roars of thunder. Two weeks later when I saw her for another treatment, she told me about her visit with the orthopedic physician a few days before. He asked her when she completed radiation on her hip and femur. She replied that she had not received any radiation. He looked puzzled, put her new x-ray up on the light board, and asked her again about the radiation and if it were possible she had forgotten. She told him emphatically that radiation treatments are not anything she would have forgotten, and then he responded with a question of how it could be possible that two weeks ago her femur was hanging on by a thread, and now there is new bone and it looked significantly improved. When she told me that story, I asked if she was kidding me and she said absolutely not. We both looked at each other, our eyes began to get misty, and I said, in my lovely vulgar way of expressing myself, "Well fuck—that's my sign. Let's do this!" She and I met at least weekly for over a year, and when we finished on that last day, when my hours were completed and we knew the treatments were over, she was really sick when I left her house, and I was thrilled. I had expected this for months. She vomited and had diarrhea for a day, and she emailed me the day after, telling me that she woke up feeling as good as she did before she was diagnosed! All the integrative and conventional therapies had worked—not forever—but she was cancer free for a bit. She had a party with some friends to celebrate, and as I sat next to her and hugged her, I knew that this journey would be one of the most precious of my lifetime.

I had another incredible experience a couple of years after. As I've said, I have a personal relationship with Jesus, but at this time, our communication was still only one way. A dear friend of mine had a brother who was diagnosed with metastatic esophageal cancer. As a gift to him, she gave him Reiki treatments with me. I saw him weekly for months. We developed a very special relationship, and I shared a great deal of my thoughts and beliefs with him. At first, being very Catholic he was skeptical, but as time progressed, he became increasingly more open to what resided on the other side of the veil. The most extraordinary experience doing Reiki to date was with him one evening. About ten minutes into our sixty-minute session, he raised both arms straight in the air. I couldn't tell if he was sleeping or in another state of consciousness—but it didn't matter. I knew immediately that someone was there with us—someone divine. I was at his head, acting as a conduit to the universal white light. As clear as a bell, I could see (with my mind's eye) and hear Jesus at the other end of the table at my client's feet. My eyes began to tear, and I froze for a moment, then I just kneeled. I heard Jesus say, "If you are so compelled to kneel, then so will I." Shortly after, we both stood back up and we remained silent with my client's arms stretched up to the heavens for a total of twenty minutes. I can't even fathom the extent of healing that occurred in those twenty minutes. I would have loved to see him cured, but he transitioned to do great things in accordance with his plan. It's pretty difficult for me to hold my arms up like that for two minutes, let alone twenty. That experience was miraculous. After the treatment I asked him what happened and how he felt during the treatment. He told me he felt like he was floating and was surrounded by love. I could not wait to share what I saw and heard with him and his wife. At first, they were shocked to think we could have been worthy of such a visit—but that's when I learned that we are all worthy of what is accessible to everyone through love.

When integrative therapies work hand in hand with conventional treatment, the results are often greatly enhanced. My clients always liked to spend time talking with me after their treatment, and I learned a lot about them and some of the stress and baggage they were chronically carrying. This helped me gain a deeper understanding of human frailty and resilience. It allowed me to gather a more acute awareness of the effects of fear, anger, resentment, and overall clutter in a person's life. It also led me to become a heart-centered hypnotherapist. I knew if I could help people unlock some of the subconscious baggage they were carrying, it could help them heal. There is so much within us that we are not consciously aware of—from in utero memories to events that happened well before our memories of this lifetime became seeded within our conscious awareness. We have developed many opinions about ourselves and other people that we don't realize. When our subconscious mind is accessed, these memories often explain issues that sabotage our current health or happiness. Just the recognition of these issues causes deep healing. More about this topic to follow, but suffice it to state right now that the extraordinary experiences were incredible and left an indelible imprint on my mind and spirit.

One person's spiritual journey can never be compared to another as we are all doing the best we can with what we have to work with, inside and out. Different people need different things. It's helpful if a person is open-minded about the structure they have believed in all their lives should their journey ignite questions within their heart and soul that negate some of those teachings. Moments of uncertainty only provide a mechanism for deeper communication with the divine—a communication that is not about talking but listening; a communication that does not include a litany of learned prayers designed for adulation or intercession but a dialog of the most intimate kind, between best friends to feel and know the truth that is sought. There are no secrets, and truth is truth. There is only one truth, and it is available to everyone—anytime and anywhere.

There is no religion on the other side, per se. There is only love. Religions are institutions, establishments, corporations, programs, rules, doctrines, dogmas, recommendations, and traditions that have been established for humankind by humankind. They are among the structures of our existence. Having said that, they serve a marvelous and miraculous purpose on earth and should therefore always be respected and honored. One should never judge another's connection to Source, as some of the closest friendships and most personal relationships to God are not visible to the outside and don't include public expression or participation in an organized religion. On the other side, people still have access to these traditions and continue learning and growing through the opportunities that exist there. It's likely difficult to fathom from an earthy perspective, so a person may need to step outside of their humanness and stretch from their comfort zones in an attempt to comprehend this information.

Our Creator would never create anything that had the slightest potential to separate humans from each other or our divine beginning. That is the work of people, not God. There is great sadness that has resulted from religions when spirituality is absent. We see it in religious wars and a lack of tolerance with diversity. There is incredible control and manipulation that has resulted in the name of religion. There is also a magnitude of deceit that resides within religions—but that is all put there by people. For millennia, there has been fighting and prejudice among many individuals, communities, states, and countries based on the competition of who or what group possesses the correct or superior belief system. There is great variation among dogmas, and where there is variation there is a lack of truth. Truth is truth. Love is truth. Love is authentic. The difference between religion and spirituality is that religion is external and spirituality is internal. Religion operates via a structure of guided beliefs, requirements, guidelines, dogmas, traditions, and a charter of behavior and operations. Religion is a belief structure, a system of faith and worship that exists externally, and spirituality is a journey within that reflects the connection between an individual, their Creator or Source, and all that is divine. Religions were established with relatively good intentions.

Many powerful individuals have lived and assisted in the creation of what they thought were recipes for salvation, happiness, peace, justice, and so on. In the past and in the modern day, many of these created infrastructures have helped the sick, abandoned, and less fortunate. Religious organizations and affiliations have provided healing, medical care, food, shelter, education, emotional support, and guidance and they have an important place in our world, past, present and future. There have been many spectacular souls who have sacrificed their independence and dedicated their lives to a spiritual or religious vocation whereby they decided to closely align their will with the will of the Creator, within the structure of their religious and spiritual beliefs. There is so much goodness that has resulted from these organized religions, even if some of that goodness rests behind the shadows of those human beings whose intentions were self-serving and took advantage of the small or weak.

On the other side, there are many ascended masters and enlightened souls who remain nameless to humankind, as humans have no awareness of their existence or their level of ascension because these souls were not popular in the same way the more well-known masters and saints were. Their anonymity is irrelevant to them, for they savor the love that envelops them. Favor is not shown to one soul over another, and all privileges (for lack of a better word) and level of divine access are based on each soul's vibration of love. The same opportunity exists for all souls, as each and every soul was created from the same source of love. There is no heaven, purgatory, or hell back home. There are only layers and layers of love, as heaven is not a place, it's a vibration. There is also density and darkness related to the absence of love. We should all strive to vibrate to the highest possible level while on earth, as that is what will accompany us home to the other side where it all began.

Perhaps this is a good time to interject that there are also angelic and galactic beings and celestial energies who originated from different star clusters that support people on earth. There are many, and an example are the Pleiadians. They are a collective of multidimensional spirit beings who assist in the process of spiritual transformation for humanity. There are channels across the world who communicate with various beings of light and bring information to us from them to assist humanity and the planet in the ascension to higher levels of vibration and consciousness. There are others—but I will refrain from further discussion since I'm not an expert and the topic falls outside the objectives of this book. That concept may be too far off the edge of the envelope, and I don't want any skepticism to minimize the truths given to me to write this book.

Each day, humankind learns more about our external existence than was known the day before, and the opportunities for spiritual growth are vast. More people are inquiring within, and there have been dramatic shifts in celestial energy patterns, solar flares, and planetary evolution. Light workers all over the globe continue to evolve from a third-dimensional mindset into a fifth-dimensional mindset where we have an inner knowing that we are one. There is progression of the soul into 6D, 7D, 8D, or even a 9D mindset. Each enrichment of vibration results in greater levels of intuition, manifestation, and spiritual gifts. There are numerous channels of divine beings, and if you explore this deeper, you may find information that really resonates within you.

Discernment is part of a higher level of consciousness. Discernment is not judgment—it is the ability to reveal your truth and develop self-mastery. One of the pillars of self-mastery is self-discipline or self-control. The only people we can control are ourselves. The time has come to unite our spirits for the good of the whole. If everyone just effectuated change in their own sphere of existence by being the love that needs to be put forth into the world, slowly we would improve the lives of many. The goal is not to know about God, it is to know God, from the inside out, not the outside in. It is to know that we are love and that unconditional love is an act of being, not of doing. All the structure, literature, dogmas, rules and regulations in the world cannot render this enlightenment as it is truly an inside job.

Everyone has the same advantages and opportunities that humankind did over two thousand years ago to connect to spirit and hear messages directly. One of the wonderful attributes about life today is that people can talk about their mystical occurrences and messages from the other side, and they won't be shunned or hanged as witches, rebels, or heretics. We are blessed to be alive in these times of great changes and awakenings.

"It is foolish to be convinced without evidence, but it is equally foolish to refuse to be convinced by real evidence."
—*Upton Sinclair, American novelist, journalist, social critic, and political activist (1878–1968)*

Chapter Six

Healing from Loss: Know No Death

One of the most difficult challenges in life is loss. Fear of loss is real, and it comes in many varieties. Loss of love, loss of health, loss of a loved one, loss of an embryo or fetus, loss of youth or a youthful appearance, loss of movement, loss of material possessions, and loss of wealth are just a few. The sadness and heartache of loss are not just associated with someone you love dying, although that can be one of the most difficult situations to accept. Even when we are happy for a loved one when they transition home to peace and joy, it's difficult for those left on earth to continue without them. Being diagnosed with a challenging or terminal illness creates emotions that many of us can only imagine. The contemplation of a treatment journey and outcome can test a person's resilience at maximum throttle, and the level of ensuing anxiety and fear can be debilitating. Living with chronic pain can present as a fate worse than death for those who suffer every minute of every day. Healing from loss—the loss of people, health, things, and so on—can seem to go beyond the definition of challenging. Living with loss requires us to look deep within ourselves to try to see the potential opportunities that reside within these challenges and to contemplate the reason or reasons the situation exists. Why would we put such challenges into our life plan, and what do we need to find within ourselves to cope? These are not easy or simple answers, and the only person who can truly help us figure it out—utilizing every resource of support possible—is ourselves. It's important to remember, however, that everything we need to cope and successfully navigate our challenges resides within us. It's an old saying, but so true—we are not given more than we can handle.

The perspective that death does not exist is paramount to accepting the death of those we love—those people and pets that really mean the world to us, but also the potential of our own death. In every case, knowing that death does not exist for the soul is paramount in acceptance. The fundamental emotion of loss is fear. Fear is real, whether it is rational or not. Fear of losing someone we love—even decades before it occurs—is not uncommon. One could argue that the fundamental emotion driving this is love, but it's not—it is fear. It's fear of loss because of the love we share with others.

My mother was often ill when I was very young. She suffered from terrible headaches and lethargy. It was not uncommon for her to tie a rolled dishcloth on her head so she could tighten it to apply pressure to ease the pain in her head. After a couple of years of this, on occasion, I would hear mumbling from adults, when they didn't know I was listening, that her pain may be psychosomatic. That made me sad and angry because I never doubted her pain. I was around her enough to know she was not faking. I loved her more than anyone or anything else in my life at that time, and I trusted her. After her diagnosis, I wanted to imagine those people's faces when they found out she had a brain tumor the size of a golf ball in her head—down deep I hoped they felt remorseful for their lack of trust and belief in her. Because I was often fearful of my mother's death, due to her state of being, I would have nightmares when I was young, and I would wake up and run to her room (I think I was about five or six years old). I would wake her up and beg her not to die. I often wonder what she must have thought to have her little girl cry and beg her not to die when she had no idea when that event would transpire but knew something was off and didn't feel well. We are products of our emotions, and we build highways of thought built on the law of association. I know that my subconscious mind, through repetition, built a highway programmed to fear the death and loss of those meaning the world to me. After my mother's death, I worried about my grandma, my mother's mother, dying for many years prior to her death. When she died at ninety-four, I was happy for her. She lived a tough but good life, and she taught me things that nobody else could have in the years I had her before and after my mother died. When she was getting ready to transition, her indomitable spirit was still present, and I had no doubt, as in life, she was in total control of that transition. The last time I saw her was five days before her death. When we said goodbye, she said, "Now don't you worry about a thing," and she winked at me. I was thirty when she died, and she was one of my greatest gifts in this lifetime, especially because my personality is similar to hers—mix in some of my dad and my mom, and that explains almost everything!

It was interesting that one day, shortly after my mother died, I was hanging in my dad's room chatting with him and he looked at me and said, "Are you worried I'll die?" It was as if he was reading my mind! I said, yes, and he replied, "I'm going to live a long, long time, and you don't have to worry about me dying. You'll be old yourself!" He died at ninety-six when I was sixty years old (not old!). I totally believed him and never had a doubt after he told me he wasn't going anywhere for a long time. When he did transition, I knew his physical body was ready for the adventure, and I accepted it with a loving heart.

My brother really spent the most time with my dad in the years before his death, caring for him in a nursing home. Unfortunately, my dad's greatest nightmare of being in a nursing home came true, and there wasn't anything any of us could do about it as his lack of mobility prohibited him from being at home. When we were alone, he told me that he didn't have an iota of fear about dying, but he did worry about the process. He wasn't interested in suffering and prolonging the inevitable when the time came. Since I've been in healthcare my whole career and I was so active in our community, I developed some wonderful friendships, and I was confident they would become resources for us when needed. I assured him I'd make sure he passed as quickly and comfortably as possible. About two weeks before he died, my older brother, my stepmother, and I were hanging out in his room chatting. He knew it wasn't going to be long before he died. I asked him if he had seen my mother yet. He replied no—he had seen his sister and others but not her. I reiterated all the things I had told him for months about his transition and what awaited him on the other side. He repeated, "I hope you're right," several times. Everything I shared with him is in this book, as well as *A Human's Purpose*. After about the fourth time he said, "I hope you're right," I told him I wanted him to promise me something. I asked him to get a message to me after he died and just say, "You were right." He looked at me rather puzzled and replied, "Well, if I can." I assured him he would see a way as there were several options I knew would be available to him. I made him promise three times.

The Wednesday before he died, I was chatting with my

brother while he was in my father's room. I had discussed the palliative process with the physician who was the medical director of the nursing home. He was a wonderful and agreeable physician and assured me he would make sure my father was comfortable and would die peacefully. When I spoke to my brother that day, I could hear my dad speaking loudly and saying, "Help me . . . help me!" I asked my brother what was going on and I told him that the situation was unacceptable. I hung up and called an incredible physician who I had a great relationship with who was the medical director of our hospice—an organization where I spent twelve years as a board member and chair. She told me the drug regimen that would allow my dad to transition without all that anxiety, confusion, and discomfort. Although the dosages were those used by oncologists and palliative care specialists, the regime of morphine and Ativan were higher than most primary care physicians use. When I spoke to the medical director of the nursing home and explained, however, he was completely amenable to the regime change and instituted it immediately. My brother said that after the new regime of drugs, my dad was quiet and comfortable within two hours. He died very peacefully on Sunday.

On the Tuesday after, I received a text message from a dear man who is one of the most respected spiritual leaders in our community. He is in constant communication with his spiritual mentor—the master with whom he spent many years under tutelage in India. He knew my father died because I posted the obituary on Facebook. He knew nothing of my dad's and my discussions, promises, or details of his death. This is the text message written exactly how I received it on my phone:

My dear sister—you are all wrapped in the Light of Love. Your dad is literally beaming—"you were right," no father could be so blessed to have a daughter who not only makes him proud on a worldly plane, but who literally could guide my transition to the next. I am free. Always with you in love and spirit—miss being able to hug you.

When I received the text, I almost fell out of my chair. I responded that he would never know how much it meant to me, and his reply was simply, "Babaji wanted to make sure you received it." You can imagine what those I share this story feel, especially my stepmother who was listening intently at the directions I gave my dad prior to his death. This story has brought peace to whomever I share it with—whether they were dealing with a terminal illness or experienced the loss of a loved one.

The vulnerability of this type of loss comes from a place of love, because we are only vulnerable when we love someone or a pet so much that we don't want to imagine our life without them. I suppose having this firsthand experience of fear and trepidation for so many years from when I was five or six to when my mother died at when I was fourteen has built some highways of thought built on that law of association that are hard for me to let go. With all my maturity and whatever level of self-mastery I have achieved, sometimes the vulnerabilities and scenarios I create within myself are irrational, yet they creep into my conscious awareness. I try very hard to eliminate those thoughts and replace them with love and peace because I don't want to create any self-fulfilling prophesies or have those thoughts float into the ether. This takes self-discipline and sometimes we need to compartmentalize irrational beliefs of all kinds and ignore them or give them to divine beings to resolve for us. We need to trust our co-created plans as well as the co-created plans of others. We just need to love ourselves and others and accept assistance from the army of light that protects and guides us.

As my dad would say, "Maryann, we are all going to die someday." When he was in his nineties, he told me that living a long time is great, but you must be willing to experience the death of many you love. He lived longer than most of his siblings and all his best friends, and I know watching them die and experiencing their deaths could not have been easy, but he never lost his great attitude, sense of humor, or level of happiness to be alive.

Goodbyes are really important. If we have the ability to say goodbye with no regrets, immersed in love, that's a true gift. Everyone should make every effort to create the conditions for a beautiful goodbye when they know a transition is near. On my fourteenth birthday in June, my mother lost her balance and fell. My dad took her to the emergency room as she hit her head and needed stitches. Every detail of that night when I flew out of bed will be carved into my memory. Shortly after, her neurosurgeon thought perhaps her brain tumor was back. In the end, the tumor had not grown back, she had just lost her balance. She died because of repeated surgeries to move the shunt in the head to minimize swelling. The whole summer was spent on this roller coaster. She was in the hospital for months. She died in November from septicemia. Because the diagnostic tools we have today were yet to be discovered in 1973, and we didn't have the powerful antibiotics we have today, an infection overran her body, diseased her blood, and caused her death. Since she was in the hospital for so long, it was likely that this was a nosocomial infection with a highly resistant microbe she acquired during her stay. It's hard to fathom that she had to undergo the entire testing and surgical process again. This time I was old enough to know exactly what was happening. I got my working papers shortly after my fourteenth birthday. I started working as a candy striper so I could spend time with her while she was hospitalized. I used to take a bus from near my home, transfer to another bus downtown, and volunteer at the hospital. I'd see her periodically throughout the day and spent each evening I was there with her until my dad would arrive and I'd catch my ride home with him. One day during that summer when my dad and I were hanging out with my mom, a nurse came into her room and said, "You know honey, you're really not supposed to be here, you're not sixteen years old." I replied, "Well you see, almost every day I'm here in patients' rooms delivering flowers or mail or selling candy or newspapers. If you think it's OK for me to be in every patient's room all day long and not my mother's, you are free to carry me out, as that would be the only way I'm leaving!" Every now and then my dad would remind me of that story. Suffice it to say, the nurses all welcomed me with open arms after that, showed me where their break room was, and allowed me to make toast and eat anything that was available. When my mother was in the ICU, however, just prior to her death, I visited her. When I was walking out, the nurse told me that I really shouldn't be there as I wasn't sixteen. I agreed and told her I would not visit again. My dad used to tell me that's when he knew that I couldn't take it anymore—but that wasn't the case at all. There were two reasons. First, I wasn't old enough and I agreed. There were no candy stripers in the ICU. The second and most important reason is because my mother and I had a storybook goodbye. One that fills my heart and soul with love and joy to this day. I did not want any other encounter to ruin or pollute that goodbye—I insisted within myself that it was the most perfect goodbye, never to be replaced.

Since most of us don't know when we will die, we should make every goodbye count like it could be the last.

Everyone should also try to heal and forgive any clutter that resides within that is a result of hate, disappointment, anger, or resentment toward another person. That clutter does nothing to hurt the other person or change the situation. Forgiveness provides internal and eternal freedom. Freedom from the bondage that those negative thoughts create. Freedom to transition without baggage so our souls and spirits can more swiftly proceed through ascension, and our transition can be made more easily because we will be lighter (literally and figuratively due to a higher vibration of love and light)! The key to processing death is to truly know that we do not lose anyone. People and pets we love simply experience a change of form. They will always have access to us if we continue to welcome them into our lives. Both sides can feel love, know memories, and assist each other. Only one side, however, has the easier time of being in many locations at one time, walking through walls, and having an eagle-eye view of anything they desire. If you don't believe me, find an excellent medium and invite your loved ones to speak to you. Open your mind and heart and let it be. I have known so many who have had a life-altering experience when they experience "know no death." Neither time nor space can interfere with that loving communication and bond.

I will share my first experience with an incredible medium that occurred when I was twenty-eight years old. I was married without children, and I supervised a microbiology department at a veterans administration medical center. I had known others who went to psychics before, and I was not interested in hearing the future. As an aside, because we live in the land of free will, nobody can predict the future with certainty. An individual with these types of gifts can provide information about the future that is aligned or consistent with a current situation, but only what is applicable at that moment in time. The fabric of our circumstances is malleable and changes with the thoughts and decisions that people make over whom we have no control. The information is always fascinating, but nobody should bank on that info and get their heart set on anything in the future.

Back to the story—a laboratory technologist from another department was telling me about her mother's furnace and what a gift it was to find out where her dad kept some important information and spare parts for its maintenance. I stopped her and said, "Isn't your father dead?" To which she answered, "Yes, but we spoke to him through this incredible medium." You know what came next—I asked for her phone number!

When I finally arrived for a reading—she was hard to get an appointment with, and it took months—I was beyond excited. I had now lived as long on the earth with my mom in the flesh as I had with her in spirit. When the reading started, the medium was telling me things that were insignificant. She paused and asked if I had any questions, and I replied, "Yes—is my mother here?" She replied, "Yes. She followed you in here and can't believe she can speak to you, but she's crying too hard to speak, and if she starts speaking, I will cry, then you will cry, and we won't get anyplace!" Honestly, I wanted to jump out of my seat! With conviction and a bit of snarky, I said, "Mom—are you KIDDING ME! After fourteen years you are going to mess up this opportunity! Think of something else and stop crying!" The medium replied, "Oh your mom is laughing, and she said, "OK, how is Wanda?" Now my mother loved this woman, Wanda—she was my sister-in-law's mother. I loved her too, but she was the least likely person to be in my thoughts. I said, "Mom—really? Fourteen years, and your first question is how is Wanda?" The medium said my mother began to laugh and replied, "Well, you told me think of something else, and she was the person who popped in my head!" A few things happened here—most importantly, there was no doubt in my mind that my mother was in that room. I realized that laughing, crying, and the myriad of emotions, thoughts, advice, and most importantly love were but a breath away. I also realized my mother was still my mother. She maintained the same personality and memories, along with knowledge of everything that had occurred since her death. My life was forever changed, and my self-mastery journey began. My mother told me things nobody else could know—and she even reminded me of funny things I used to do when I was a kid about which I had to seek confirmation from my father. So, for those who think the medium was just reading my mind, there was info she knew that wasn't in my mind to read! There was also no Google, so for the skeptics, I don't think she went to the library and researched me either! My mother gave me some idea of what her life was like on the other side, and she recommitted her love, pride, and constant companionship and assistance, as she had promised before she died. The medium also told me things that would not happen for many years in the future—things I thought were crazy and didn't give much thought! She told me I'd be a vice president of some medical facility, and I would write books—I didn't believe I could do that, but as it turns out, I did. It must be that I made the decisions and choices that were aligned with my co-created plan. I became a VP of one of our acute care hospitals at thirty-six years old, and my first book was published in 2012 when I was fifty-three . . . now that's looking into the future since I was twenty-eight when she provided these insights! I have always tried to listen to spirit and allow them to illuminate the path that recognized all my gifts and potential and allowed me to use them to the best of my ability.

As a society we make every effort to keep people alive. Physicians put forth great effort to help people live their longest and best lives. They do it within the stresses of our unsustainable healthcare system, increasing costs, and diminishing revenue, coupled with noncompliant patient behavior, escalating levels of obesity, and poor life choices. Outside of our healthcare system, I'd like to say that I think the culture of our country is to keep people healthy and help them live their longest and best life, but it's not. The culture of our country is to make money, which allows many self-serving opportunists to flourish. I find it very hard to trust most information. The best source of truth is yourself—from within. We all have superpowers that can access the wisdom of our higher self, the collective consciousness and divinity. It's called body dowsing or, most recently, quantum physics. Quantum physics is home to studies like quantum mechanics, quantum statistics, quantum electrodynamics, and quantum field theory. Over the last several decades, exploration in quantum field theory has led to a broad range of new ideas and tools. String theory and quantum field theory have provided information about space-time. Space-time is a system that looks at four dimensions—one temporal and three spatial coordinates. It studies situations and objects at an atomic or subatomic level. Every day science substantiates ideas, skills, and techniques that are thousands of years old. It's important, however, to blend contemporary wisdom with holistic modalities. By themselves, neither is optimal. Most people look for the easy road—the magic bullet to maintain or regain health. Others work very hard to balance everything in their life to promote wellness. Either way, most of us want to escape death and live. As precious as the end-of-life journey is to accompany somebody you love, it's not an easy ride. It's often difficult for those with a terminal illness to register with hospice, as the "H" word usually signifies death, and some do not want to have any association with that designation. Sadly, opportunities to help caregivers can be missed because of that philosophy.

You can add me to the list of people who work hard to defy age and create the conditions for healthy living and aging. I love seeing ninety- and one-hundred-year-old runners breaking world records! I'd love to run a 5K and set a world record at one hundred years old. I have no idea whether it's a realistic desire, but I put it on my bucket list, so I'm trying to create the conditions for that goal to be possible! Having said that, nobody knows how long we have on this planet, so we need to enjoy the precious moments we have and always be prepared to go back home to the other side. We create the conditions here and now for how our soul will exist on the other side. It behooves us to clear the clutter within and purify our spirits with love. The object to winning the game of life is to vibrate at the highest frequency we can, resolve any past life issues that continue to rear their ugly heads, and prepare for the gifts of eternal love. The journey of life should never be motivated by fear, but by love. As we continue to live, so must we enrich our self-discipline and our self-mastery.

Using love at the motivator, we must identify what is most important to ourselves—not the minute-by-minute importance but the long game. For example, if my long game is to be healthy, I have to determine what elements of my life will get me to healthy living. The components I have identified for myself are deep spirituality, immersion in love, healthy eating, movement and exercise, and stress reduction. Running fulfills my desire for deepened spirituality because I spend hours with the spirit world while I run (this includes the God within). It fulfills my immersion in love because I love nature, and I run outside without music to spend time listening to the sounds of the land. Running also fulfills my exercise and movement goal, and it reduces my stress. The return on my running investment is, therefore, high. It's silly to think that I don't need to motivate myself or push myself to run when I'm tired or just not in the mood. I push myself all the time. I push to heal myself from injuries, often at the admonishment of others. Why? Because my long game—my ultimate goal of healthy living and aging—is not based upon what I want now, it's based upon what I want most. So, I get my running shoes on and push myself, or I eat a quarter of the donut instead of the whole thing, or I have ten peanut M&Ms instead of the bag, because it's not what I want at that moment, it's what I want most for the long haul. I guess you could say that's a form of self-discipline because we know most of life is all mental. It's the games you play with yourself to keep your eye on the prize. Hey, I'm just as sad as the next guy when those M&Ms are gone—but I wouldn't be less sad after the bag, I'd probably be sad and sick as my glucose levels would soar and then the drop and make me feel like crap. It's not worth the bag. You have to say goodbye to the M&Ms sooner or later. I try to pick sooner as it's in my best interest and is consistent with my long-term objectives. I'll also add that sometimes you just need to eat the whole bag and forgive yourself—but the last time I did that was on my sixteenth birthday!

If we could visit the other side and remember how awesome it is, I wonder if people's thoughts about dying would change. Can you imagine a world where people are thrilled for those who will pass to the other side? Can you imagine being excited for others when they are dying? We would always be sad for ourselves—those left behind—

but we will see them again, and while they are dead, they will be with us. It would be very selfless to let them go with a happy send-off, putting our feelings of loss and sadness aside for love.

As long as the planet has housed thinking humans, it has contained variations in opinions and beliefs, and adversity has continually resulted from differences in thought. Some people are afraid of dying because of the religious beliefs or falsities that have been engrained in their subconscious and conscious minds. Some feel they are not worthy of the gifts of heaven. The goal is to use our free will to seek truth and light while traveling through the maze of life to find the one true light and understand that it illuminates from within and connects us all to each other and all that is divine. There is so much we don't know! We also don't know what we don't know!

Over a century ago, Albert Einstein predicted that gravitational waves existed, and in October 2017, an event was detected in space that had never been seen before, but it occurred 130 million light-years ago. It was a fiery collision of two neutron stars that created a cloud of radioactive waste the size of our solar system. David Shoemaker, a senior MIT research scientist at the time, explained that it was filled with a magnitude of precious metals—gold and platinum. It solved a long-standing mystery in astrophysics regarding where these precious metals come from. Although an event like this had never been seen before in human history, it very closely resembled predictions that scientists had been making. It doesn't mean it never happened before—it just means people on earth didn't know it. We don't know a lot of things on planet earth. That's part of the joy—discovering, uncovering, predicting, proving, and disproving.

On the other side, there are those souls that practice

the religious traditions they held close to their hearts before they died. It makes many feel comfortable in that familiarity and gives them a more solid connection to their family and friends on earth. Many on the other side encourage and appreciate prayers from the living, and they return those prayers and intercession to those on earth. Prayer is a frequency of love and care that allows love energy to transcend dimensions and be felt in any spectrum of existence. Prayer has great power, as the intentions and energy are fueled by love. Love never ceases to command the universe or our existence. Many on the other side find comfort in praying, as they did when they occupied human form. They love when those on earth remember them, pray for their well-being, and ask for intercession from those on the other side that humans consider to be saints or masters. All expressions of love can assist a soul in a variety of ways and capacities.

Many souls have an insatiable desire to explore a greater and more robust understanding of love, religions, the mystics, and how the whole enchilada came about—there is so much information on the other side about everything. There is a magnitude of history, scientific discoveries made and yet to be made, mathematical equations yet to be understood by the human mind, and so much more. Contemplation and prayer are as important on the other side as they are on earth. Among other benefits, prayers offer mantras that can calm the mind and body and assist in the building of resiliency on earth. Saying the rosary can be one of the best uses of time for those who love the history and energy of those prayers. Sitting quietly, connecting to spirit, and listening, with wide eyes like the wonder of a child, can be life altering. Learning how to harness the love and light within and illuminate the world has great impact for all souls. As Yoda says in *Star Wars*, "You must unlearn what you have learned."

If we truly understood what awaits on the other side, death would take on a different flavor for everyone. The incredible opportunities to expand soul awareness, knowledge, and wisdom on the other side are unfathomable to most of us on earth. These blessings offer hope to the bereaved and those loved ones who are in the process of transitioning to death. There are many schools of learning, universities, and lectures given by masters who have changed the landscape of our existence on the other side. There are also libraries that hold the history of the galaxies and any information past, present, and to some extent future that a soul could want to know. There's a hall of records for each soul so they can explore their lifetimes and the Akash with co-created plans and witness the progression of their soul evolution. The opportunities are endless. Many select jobs, travel, and spend time with those they loved on earth. Opportunity abounds with just sincere desire, love, and gratitude. Some souls take on roles to be guides or stewards of greater learning and invention by hanging close enough to the earth plane or dimension to help inspire and precipitate new discoveries. There are opportunities to perfect musical talents, voice lessons, choir (naturally)—there is nothing not to love about the other side or back home. That's why it's so hard to leave, and even though most people have amnesia, at some level of consciousness everybody knows it. Sometimes the separation causes great internal struggle and strife—and people don't know why they are all mixed up inside. Many travel back home during sleep and continue their studies then too. It often helps with the resolution to mathematical problems, science, construction, emotional turmoil, life's challenges—you name it. It is truly a frequency—or place in human terms—to love! There are no secrets, but with a higher vibration comes greater access to information. The more you recognize you are love, the higher you vibrate! It's not to create layers or classes or levels of souls or to be snotty or hold back information, but a soul that is not ready to receive information can suffer if it is exposed to something it does not understand or is not ready to receive. It's pretty simple and everyone accepts it in the spirit of love that it is intended. There are many doors to enter our Creator's castles.

Soul growth is through love, love through experience, recognition, acceptance, and gratitude and love through adversity, anger, frustration, and disappointment. When the soul is released from the human vehicle, it returns to where it came from. A child of God, returning to God finally has the self-realization in their sacred heart to remove every fictitious and man-made assumption of the self that was magnetized through beliefs and intentions created through lifetimes. On earth, guilt often prevents a person from deviating from their original path or belief system when they begin to question the potential existence of a flawed premise or they begin to explore new ways of developing their spiritual connection with Oneness.

The mystery of life is that God is present in each one of us, in everything, everywhere, within this a tapestry of Oneness on planet earth. We are a miracle made of love, living each day to recognize that the power we seek to live, embrace, and overcome challenge and cope with the difficult terrain is within. We are given free will to evolve, to make our own decisions, and to grow from each celebration or redirection. Free will is not an authorization to behave badly without regard for consequence. Free will provides the power and privilege to co-create life, to continually review life, revise it as needed, and reinvent ourselves to become better people than we were the day before. Free will allows for personal growth and can underscore the privilege and responsibility that comes with being love. Humans have the freedom to choose, and this freedom would have no meaning without rights; the directions a person selects for themselves would have no value and provide no growth without the freedom and ability to choose.

"We are all part of the One Spirit. When you experience the true meaning of religion, which is to know God, you will realize that He is your Self, and that He exists equally and impartially in all beings."
—Paramahansa Yogananda

Chapter Seven

Our World of Structure

As humans, we are immersed in a world of structure. We are affected significantly by time. Most of us use our alarm clocks to wake up at a certain time, and we continue to keep track of time throughout the day to adhere to schedules and fulfill whatever responsibilities are on deck for the day. Even the homebound and retired likely watch TV and pay attention to time regarding their meals and favorite programs or movies. Time has been created to keep order, and frankly, I can't live without my watch, but in the spirit world, time does not exist.

While driving on the road, there are structured laws and rules of conduct that are mandatory. We go to school or work in organizations that are structured as legal entities with structured charters of operation. We have structured organizational missions/values/visions, organizational charts and job descriptions that outline each employee's roles and responsibilities. Organizations of religious affiliation are structures with dogmas and codes of conduct. There are usually physical structures that accommodate the religions' place of worship. There is a structure of how and when these places of worship operate. There are educational structures in the form of schools, colleges, and universities with structured parameters for admission and teaching. Many of us adhere to home or business budgets, ensuring the structure of our financial health can sustain our needs. Whether we like it or not, structure is all around us, and every minute of every day we are doing something to fit into the structure that is necessary for our continued existence, well-being, and success.

Money provides the means to create and sustain our structures. Money does not buy happiness, but it buys food, shelter, safety, and the necessities of daily living. When there is enough money to cover what is needed, the additional funds can provide what is wanted. Sometimes what is wanted is modest and sometimes it's ostentatious. Sometimes when people have an excess of money, the fear of losing it or just wanting more money becomes a catalyst for needing an expanding, continuous surplus. Money can be allowed to become the fundamental driver that dictates many or most of those individuals' decisions, and money becomes the driver of the bus instead of grateful cargo.

There are structured or accepted norms and paradigms of living. There are structured expectations and judgment. There are people who cannot survive in the structure that mankind has developed, and with time, they crave an exit strategy—whether consciously or not. Some may opt for suicide, or their constant level of stress or unhappiness causes such internal distress that it catalyzes dis-ease to create an exit strategy that develops from the inside out.

Part of living a joy-filled life is having the resilience and fortitude to understand structure, accept its existence, and allow ourselves to create the conditions for the elements of structure that serve our highest good to be sustained. Part of living a joy-filled life is having a spiritual connection, rooted in love, which allows an individual to overcome their insecurities and successfully navigate the terrain of life, knowing that unwavering support and unconditional love is their birthright. When all the eggs are in the structure basket, there is always the risk of collapse. When somebody spends all their time running on the hamster wheel of fortune, ensuring their structure of wealth is sustained, they often start to confuse priorities. When this continues over an extended period, they may forget whatever their priorities were and lose themselves in structure. It is not uncommon, in time, for these individuals to feel that there is a void in their life as they realize they love their plethora of things, but they are still not happy and can't really figure out how to be happy.

We know happiness is an inside job. Basic needs in life must be met, but how we look at life and how we think creates our existence. This includes the level of investment we have in structure, and if that investment in structure supersedes our investment in love, in spirit, and in ourselves.

In the summer of 2024, I trained for the New York City marathon that took place in November. It was an unusually hot and humid summer in Central New York. There were enough days over ninety degrees to make it a record. It's tough to train for a race or marathon when it's hot and humid and you're sixty-five years old. I was running in my neighborhood, and I recall being so happy to escape the sun and run on a part of the street that was lined with trees and shade. I had such gratitude for the temporary relief that the shade provided. Then I thought of all the times I wasn't happy to see the shade because it was cold and I preferred the warmth of the sun to envelop my body. Then I thought the only difference in how the shade is valued from one moment to the next is me. The trees don't move—the shade has no priorities—it's all how I look at it. I thought of my self-mastery journey. I thought of how it truly is never-ending, and there's always opportunities for new thought and personal growth, even in the smallest decisions or increments. I made a promise to thank the shade when I ran through it, regardless of how it affected me—just to continue to grow in whatever way possible from this simple thought of gratitude. It does underscore that most "stuff" in life does not happen to us . . . it just happens, and we often get mixed up in the dust.

On the other side, there is an innate incentive to love and cooperate rather than judge. A desire for material possessions, power, wealth, prestige, and other such structured, egoic priorities are removed by leaving the physical world behind. We all land on the other side with the same physical properties—which are none. The baggage we take, however, is that which resides in the shadows of our being, the clutter that represents all the unresolved issues that we failed to explore, deal with, or heal. Even with free will, when the soul leaves all its human constraints behind, love matters more than anything, and its power can be witnessed and experienced instantly as the soul leaves the physical body. It's actually a reentry, not a new destination, as when we die, we remember all the times we have been there before, and we become privy to the lives we lived on earth. It's important for a human to realize and accept that how they think on earth will affect their entire body and soul, and it will have an impact on how the soul reacclimates after physical death. The indelibly intertwined physical, mental, emotional, and spiritual aspects of humanity respond to the resonance of thought, and this resonance will also affect your soul's experience back home. There is no time like the present to get a grip on how and why a person thinks the way they do and carries anger, resentment, or other negative baggage within. Thoughts are building blocks of all creations and events;

the body reacts to thoughts in visible and invisible ways. The nervous and endocrine systems were created to maintain homeostasis or balance in the human body. Thoughts affect hormones, neurohormones, and electric transmitters in the body. The body is full of electric currents as we discussed in previous chapters.

Humans have billions of receptors that constantly receive information, or perhaps I should say that they are constantly bombarded with information. The result of this union causes a cascade of biological events in our bodies that respond to thoughts, emotions, and feelings. A person can alter their physical makeup by how they think! Each cell is alive and can change depending on the signal from a receptor. This principle is known as the mind-body connection. In summary, this can be understood by acknowledging that every thought has a corresponding reaction in the body because impulses are connected by thoughts and memories built on the law of association. We become products of our emotions. Where do you feel fear—in your heart or the pit of your stomach or intestines? Where do you feel excitement—in your heart and throat? Where do you feel love—all over your body? Many fail to understand that consciousness does not reside in the brain, but in every cell of the body. Receptors associated with everything from what a human believes to what he eats expand by usage. The more sugar a person eats, the more they will crave. The more alcohol a person drinks to drown their sorrows, the more they will require, thereby fueling that habit or addiction. The more a person believes they have a dark cloud over their head that makes bad things happen, the more of the same will occur. The more one individual gives his power away and allows another to aggravate them to get their blood boiling, the easier the blood boils the next time they interact. Over time, receptors expand by usage, and humans become products of their actions and emotions. This is why it's so important to retain the power that resides within and pay attention to what we say to ourselves and others. Stress activates a variety of responses and mechanisms in the body. Everyone gets stressed, but a slow, constant burn of chronic stress can have life-altering effects. Chronic stress puts humans in a constant state of fight or flight, even if they have become comfortable with the feelings and lack awareness of this issue. Stress does things in the body like increase glucose levels, heart rate, blood pressure, and breathing. A warning to divert blood from the skin and digestive organs to skeletal muscles occurs because a body is getting prepared to run from danger to safety. An increase in adrenaline and cortisol also occurs. Adrenaline causes rapid heart and respiratory rates, and cortisol is involved in multiple bodily functions like regulating blood pressure and cardiovascular and immune functions. Nobody wants to go messing with these systems since they help maintain good health and a positive outlook on life. At least nobody wants to mess with them on purpose, but many people have health issues that result from the constant buzz of stress.

The body responds to thoughts and actions in so many ways. It is vitally important for a human to understand the cascade of effects that result from how they think and live. Humans are beings of energy. We can feel the energy from others, and the energy we exude joins with the collective energy of the whole. That's why taking a break and immersing yourself in nature can do a lot to clear the mind and de-stress an individual.

Knowingly or not, there are those who love to suffer—it connects them to earthly structure or like-minded individuals with a bond that feeds their soul. Some humans embrace a martyr-like existence. They make a career of over-coming obstacles that were inadvertently placed in their way by themselves. Some overtly express their perception of how much harder they work, how much more they do, and how much more they give than others when they really have no idea what beliefs or perceptions reside in other people's hearts and what challenges rest at others' feet. This is an example where judgment of that kind strains the love relationship and creates tighter connections with structure. It's not uncommon for humans who continually survive their various misfortunes to allow that survival to become the basis for their accomplishments and self-esteem. Humans should avoid any attachment between love and suffering. This tragic relationship can create a self-fulfilling prophecy that perpetuates continual suffering. It's not necessary and it is absolutely not mandated by a higher being of light, master, or God.

The universe responds to love. When love rules, structure becomes the servant, creating what is consistent with that resonance. Some are accustomed to achieving with force and action instead of magnetism and attraction. For example, many people who call themselves leaders have gained that status at the expense of others. They have used strategies like control and intimidation, and they've likely put in many hours of arduous effort—working more hours than most—because it's more difficult to work without love being the driver. When we don't cooperate with the forces of nature, it often takes much longer to get where you're going, and it can also be painful. Force and action are the drivers in that type of individual and that type of structure, but force and action do not rule the universe, love does. On the other hand, there are leaders who are loved and respected who have dedicated their lives to helping others see the best in themselves. They develop teams that have love and trust at their core. The universe has purposefully encouraged or placed that type of person in positions of leadership because they will create success via magnetism, respect, cooperation, and teamwork. They will become role models for others, and they will make the world a better place through the aggregate efforts of their teams. They and their teams will attract that which resonates with their dominant thoughts, which include the circumstances that are best for the whole—their driver being love. This is known as the principle or law of attraction. Basically, we attract people and situations that most harmonize or resonate with our dominant thoughts because energy attracts like energy. These leaders seem to be successful without trying. It can appear effortless to one looking in from the outside, but trust me, there was effort! We all know there's plenty of energy that is exerted to be successful, but I'm confident you will know what I mean if you stop and think about the people you know or know of in leadership positions who are loved by their staff or constituents. The leaders fueled by love don't need to work one hundred hours per week or sacrifice their health and well-being or time with their families. You see, they don't have to work one hundred hours per week because the universe is working with them by making the right things happen through love. It's not easy for the egoic, power-based, structurally immersed leader to redirect themselves to become a leader fueled by love, because they are solidly programmed in one direction. Often, it's not even feasible for them to accept another paradigm. They would hear this and say, "Nonsense! It's hard work, power, and control that make me successful!" When they leave behind their human vessel and take what everyone else brings back home with them, they will understand. What a nicer world it would be if everyone worked on understanding the role of spirit and structure while they were alive. It is possible to change directions, but those individuals would need to work with more spirit and less ego and alter their paradigm of leadership and life. Sometimes that takes more than one lifetime of practice.

When the human ego and structure dominate a person's free will, instead of love and spiritual intuition, structure becomes the master instead of the servant. Structure should be a servant to love, but in humanness it's easy to get magnetized by power and control. Ego is composed of self-serving self-talk and fictitious opinions that people have allowed to interfere with their constitution of self-love. Their thoughts and actions are often self-sabotaging because they come from structure and not love. The ego cares about the ego and its self-preservation. When a person's intentions are love driven instead of ego driven, life is simpler, easier, and happier. That's why it's so important to have love-based thoughts instead of ego-based thoughts, and the best way to eliminate ego-based thoughts is to minimize and eliminate fear. Fear of not looking important enough, fear of not being important enough, fear of not getting credit, fear of a lack of respect and admiration, and the list continues. Living in a space of structure, illusions, and separation from whatever form your Creator's energy takes will lead to more frustration and negativity in life. Love commands and controls everything. Like a wide-eyed child without any preconceived notions, we should seek that which resides within the recesses of our sacred heart that holds every answer and solution to our challenges.

Be love and know your presence makes a difference in this world. Be authentic and true to your calling and capacity to love and be loved. People who believe they are separate from our Creator's energy often deny that they are unconditional love because the concept escapes them. If you do believe in God, believe in the God that is not capable of creating anything but love, remembering that with this love comes free will. Free will that was granted to allow you to affect your life in accordance with your thoughts and actions, adding to the aggregate effects to the world without any divine manipulation, mandates, or prescribed occurrences. The individual soul that chooses darkness and complete separation from the Source energy is unwilling to open their heart to love and light. The love vibration would destroy evil and consume the darkness in an instant if allowed. The light would consume the darkness, and the evil would vanish in a flash. Oh, there are plenty of lost or dark souls both on planet earth and the other side, but with love and a strong connection and conviction to spirit, a person is totally protected from such contact and influence, and with love, all things are possible.

There has been much persecution on planet earth through the millennia in the name of God and religion. By this point in the book, you must realize that this is 100 percent human doing instead of human being. There is no teacher or prophet or master on the other side who would support, encourage, or foster such separation from our Source energy or our Creator. There is no prophet or master that would support dissension, hate, or cruelty. Having said that, however, they still love and support each soul and support every co-created plan, honoring everyone's ability to choose via free will and navigate the journey of life in whatever aspect they choose. The forces that promote Oneness on the planet are many, but only through the forces of light and love can the ultimate goal and freedom of the "recognition of ONE" occur.

Chapter Eight

Is It Really That Complicated?

Confusion and fear related to uncertainties, anxieties, and adversities of life create drama. Humankind through the ages has evolved and gained a vast array of wisdom and knowledge. In many ways, our lives have been made easier from the incredible inventions and scientific, technological, and medical advancements through the centuries. Today, when you think about the speed and dexterity of communication mediums and the instant access of data from continent to continent, one realizes that we have come a long way in our relatively short history. We've made our lives so much "easier" that the potential for personal gratification gets more instantaneous every day. One would think that stress levels would be reduced and happiness would become an epidemic from all the advancements and new technologies; however, we all know that's not the case. Perhaps our world is more stressed out than ever. So many are working at record speeds and still can't get all their stuff done in the hours they are given in a day. For many, their best just doesn't seem good enough, and there's stress and a trail of self-inflicted disappointment that follows them. When we don't pay attention to taking care of "the whole," stress and drama find opportunities to insert themselves into our lives. Many are forgetting to take time to breathe. I don't mean breathe, but b-r-e-a-t-h-e. The strength of the mind-body-spirit connection has a direct correlation to our health, our resilience, and our level of immunity to drama. How did our society grow so rapidly and advance so significantly that we managed to have the significance of the mind-body-spirit connection fall through the cracks?

Some people gravitate toward drama. Drama can make a person feel like they are important or needed. Drama can be a place of comfort for some, as they may be used to swimming in it so that energy and density is comfortable. For the public, drama sells. It's not unusual for media personnel to be paid by clicks, which encourages hyperbole and, in some cases, deceit. The importance of spirituality and the necessity of its integration into everything we think and do and feel needs to gain more momentum. Spirituality or the knowing that we have the power and ability to transform our lives through the innate gifts we were bestowed is a key element to infusing love and joy into our lives and minimizing drama. The treadmill of life revolves at such speeds that the stress of "being" has often caused us to neglect our spiritual needs. As populations of communities, we are inundated by information and beliefs that have limited the way we look at ourselves—our spiritual selves. Religious dogmas, handed down through the ages, are so often accepted without thought, scrutiny, or question. I'm not sure we have been encouraged to access our higher wisdom, our spiritual vision, or our ability to seek answers within ourselves instead of relying on outside influences. Scientific advances and knowledge of new aspects of physics, chemistry, biology, space, and energy continue to expand, and although a great deal of it escapes most people, science continues to teach us that many beliefs that used to reside on the edge of the envelope can now be explained by science.

It's really important to be open minded and remember that in the big scheme of things—like the age of our planet which is stated to be 4.5 billion years—it wasn't that long ago that pagans worshipped many gods and used them to explain much of their world that scientifically eluded them. Some ancient cultures, like the Romans, believed that rusted metal was punishment from the gods. Interestingly, Pliny the Elder, who was a Roman author, documented that there was a belief that the rusting of iron was a penalty from the gods because iron was used for swords and other instruments of war. This is just one example of ancient civilizations that lacked the understanding of science to explain occurrences and events. They had no idea that rust was merely the chemical reaction between iron, oxygen, and water. We can look back at so many aspects of ancient cultures and reflect upon the events of daily living that were attributable to the anger of gods or revenge that today are simply explained by science. As the years roll forward, we will continue to learn and evolve scientifically to comprehend things that are unknown today. We will see that humanity continues to create reasons and maintain beliefs that will be justified by our ignorance.

Perhaps you are familiar with the English comedian, writer, filmmaker, and actor Ricky Gervais. He was on a show eating vegan chicken wings while exploring his tolerance to extreme levels of hot and spicy. I heard him make a few statements that I found extremely interesting and rather profound. He is a professed atheist and made the comments that if all the religious books and documents were eliminated from the planet, and all the science books and documents were also eliminated, that in two thousand years, the science materials would return and say the same thing, but the religious materials would be very different. I think that's true, and it really made me stop and contemplate what I thought those religious materials would contain. The only conclusion I think would be certain is that love would be at the core of whatever was written. And actually, Ricky Gervais states that he's an atheist because nobody can prove there's a god, but I think he has a beautiful heart, and he exudes great kindness to our world and is likely more spiritual than many religious people. I have no idea what he believes about an afterlife, but in forty to fifty years I hope I bump into him on the other side because I bet he will be thrilled by his new adventure!

Through all the economic growth and prosperity of our nations, there is still war, hunger, and poverty. People killing people—neglecting the fact that we are all one, and by hurting others we hurt ourselves. Mental health challenges are at record-high levels, and suicide rates have accelerated among teens as well as adults. People are self-anesthetizing just to cope and get through another day. It's so easy to seek the silver bullet to cure whatever issue exists because clearing the clutter within—facing the injuries and scars of the past—can be overwhelmingly difficult. Not many enjoy diving into the shadows of themselves to heal the wounds of the past, but it's within those shadows that the opportunities rest. This work from the inside out is the self-mastery journey, and it is never-ending and always healing. Although our planet is abundant, the feeling of lack still permeates our people. It is most tragic that the majority of people, especially political leaders of all countries, have not yet felt the necessity for a greater level of peace and harmony on earth. Peace on the inside leads to peace on the outside. There is so much chaos in our world, the manifestations of which are caused by the cumulative sum of chaos within the hearts and minds of people. We seem to love to complicate our lives more than necessary.

What makes drama, and why are many addicted to it? I think, like everything else, the answer can be found when we look within and venture through the self-mastery journey. The human ego writes, directs, and produces the drama and, most importantly, maintains the starring role. In the ego's need to protect itself from death, destruction, or deterioration, drama becomes one of the fundamental by-products of its density. An aspect of the self in need of rehabilitation creates drama to sustain those beliefs held about the self. Fear is one of the greatest fuels for drama. When somebody has a self-image that they are not worthy of love, they will create drama that will sustain that belief. They will prove to themselves, time and time again, that they are not worthy of love. They will attract people and situations that resonate with that same energy, and they will find themselves in patterns that recur repeatedly in a life theme. Drama is also the result of a need to make ourselves feel needed and wanted. The victim oscillates between, "It can't be my fault, it's always somebody or something else," and "I am here to save the day," and when none of those circumstances can be met for whatever reason (such as nobody is willing to sit on that teeter-totter with them), victims can turn into angry people who bully others. When the road of negativity and drama becomes paved in the highway of neurons, people get into a rotation of believing that they are not good enough and nothing can change that fact as it's been proven to them over and over, and once again, they were right. They created the conditions they were most fearful of since those were the scenarios created by resonance—creating the conditions that most closely aligned with their dominate thoughts.

Regardless of how awesome we are, being liked all the

time is an irrational desire. Even the people who adore us can get a bit sick of us now and then. When we consistently seek approval or love, we end up disappointed and angry. When we're disappointed and angry, there can also be guilt or shame. Guilt or shame can be invisible masks that the drama lover wears to work out their inner dysfunctions. That will prove fruitless as the work must be done from the inside out. Bringing others into drama to make a person feel less guilty is ineffective.

The first step in breaking cycles of drama is to be aware of the patterns of drama and subsequently try to understand the origin or source of these internal beliefs that create and foster the patterns. It's helpful to explore the core beliefs or irrational conclusions about the self that precipitate these patterns.

If you are creating conditions in your life that you can control but are not happy with, get out a piece of paper and a pen. When I say control, you can't control how others feel or think. You can't control nature. You can't control death or dying. You can control how you interpret what others say and how people and life's situations make you feel. You can control how you think about nature and try to cooperate with the forces of nature. You can control how you view death and dying and how you resolve grief and loss.

Take the pen and paper and draw a line down the middle. On the left side, write a list of what you want to change in your life and what you appear to be unhappy about. On the right side (so give yourself extra space), write three ways you can change the situation or change your mind about the situation.

For example, on the left side you may write:

- I'm exhausted because I work all day and every evening we have some place to go with our children and there are no family dinners or time to talk about life and world events. I need to keep my kids in all these activities because that's what others do, and I don't want them to fall behind or miss out on anything, but I'm losing my mind. I don't get enough sleep, and we don't eat healthily and if we do, it's before the kids' bedtime, and they don't have even enough time for homework.

For example, on the right side you may write:

- The pressure to have my kids in all these activities comes from fear. I'm afraid they will not have adequate opportunities, or they will not love me enough and feel left out. I need to remember that I'm not their friend, I'm their parent. I need to look down the corridors of time and see what activities make a difference when they are adults. I can make a list with them of all we do, with the purpose of explaining the benefits to everyone of how imperative it is to achieve balance. Life is all about balance; they might as well understand its value.

- When I create the conditions for balance (so perhaps we pick two out of three activities, or three out of five activities), I know I will be happier. There will be more peace because I will change my mind about comparing us to others. The priority is our family life and work-school-activity to life balance.

- I know a happy parent makes a happier household. We can have time for dinner and communicate and not be rushed. I will make us all put our cell phones in a basket that we don't look at for one hour, so we have family time. I'm sending my children to bed and taking their phones before. Social media causes too much stress.

Let's just say this works. Let's say the children begin to understand the importance of priorities and balance, and these tools help them cope with life later as adults. Let's just say they are angry at first, but with family time and healthy food and good communication, they begin to see the benefits of these changes, and they grow in resilience from the tiny bit of adversity this may have caused them. Let's just say when they are adults, nobody will care or talk about how many activities they did after school or how many different sports they played.

This is just an example, but I hear so many people tell me they don't know how to get off the hamster wheel with these activities. Whatever the issue is, there is always a resolution. We complicate our lives. We make decisions that are not in our best interest, so we look good when compared with others. The day nobody matters more to you than yourself is the day that the well is overflowing with enough water to quench the thirst of many. Does this sound selfish? Do you put the oxygen mask on yourself first then help your child? Is that selfish, or is that the only way to ensure you'll be coherent enough to help your child grow in strength, resilience, and sound mental health?

Chapter Nine

Happiness—The Inside Job

When your feet hit the floor as you wake up, which corridor do you walk down? Do you select the path of potential or the path of limitation? Is your attitude one of happiness, neutrality, or sadness? Are you grateful for another day, or are you bitchy and miserable about your lot in life? For the most part, are you proud of your decisions to date, or are you regretful? Do you feel like you can still make choices to change your life, or is this it—are you stuck? We decide our own fate, and the answers to all these questions and more are dependent upon how we view ourselves and life rather than what is happening around us. The decision to be happy and tolerant becomes easier when we understand who we are and recognize that things are not always what they appear to be. Life is full of illusions. One of them is thinking that something or somebody other than you is responsible for your happiness. Your parents, partners, spouse, children, friends, or enemies are not responsible for your happiness. This is completely on you. If you don't like your situation, change it. If you're unhappy with your partner, separate. If you don't like where you live, move. I understand that it may not be easy, but there's always hope. Hope to modify your life with different thought patterns and actions. When we make decisions with love, honesty, courage, and accountability, things usually work out in our best interest.

Everyone has struggles and challenges, and everyone overcomes them from how they think and react. Social media offers a view of family, friends, acquaintances, and popular strangers who have magnificent lives! Sometimes it's hard for people, especially young people, to recognize that those snippets of life are merely a glimpse into a tiny fraction of their reality, or they are not even truthful representations of what's really occurring in their lives.

We are only limited by the boundaries we place on ourselves. Regardless of what's happening in life, we never lose our ability to choose. Happiness is a choice—a choice that hopefully you make every day, despite the challenges that surround you. Perhaps if you sat quietly and thought of how you can create the conditions to be happy and facilitate your daily decisions, it would be helpful. Think of the following (and feel free to get that paper and pen out again):

What does happiness feel like to you?

- Being loved: Does being loved make you happy? The best way to be loved is to love, because it is in giving that we receive. When you walk in the energy of love, it will be like a magnet that brings love your way.

- Loving others: Does loving others make you happy? There are so many ways to love others—people near and far and in between. It must, however, start with the love of self. It's close to impossible to love others if we don't love ourselves. A love exercise we can do is look in the mirror and practice loving what you're looking at—regardless of what you're thinking you look like! If someone is looking to love others more but is not sure how to expand exposure to others, there are many volunteering opportunities that will allow people to meet new people and make a difference. Don't forget our furry friends out there—pets are unconditional love at its finest.

- Tolerance and the acceptance of people and their opinions that differ greatly from yours: We don't need to agree, but we need to respect and accept. We need to accept that differences in opinion will always exist, and as these differences become vaster and more global in nature, the truth is often unattainable, as information is mixed with human ego, personal or national agendas, and individual perceptions. We also need to understand that even when the truth rests in clear view and understanding, what we see and experience is earthly. Always remember that we view life through our individual lens—a lens that is created, developed and limited from birth and is the by-product of all our life experiences to date. The universe has a mandate to rebalance that which tips the scales in a negative direction. This rebalance can be likened to karma. We don't know why others have put the burdens, struggles, and challenges into their lives that they have co-created, but our only role is to love, trust, and support. The energy of acceptance flows freely from a fundamental belief that in our lifetime, things are not always what they appear to be, and there truly is a reason for everything. Acceptance of that which negates our beliefs is easier when we acknowledge that we do not possess the complete dataset of what rests behind or ahead of us, and most importantly, the complete dataset of another individual.

Since we are the authors, producers, and directors of our lifetimes on earth, the free will planet, we create the conditions for our life, and we gather that which resonates with our most dominate thoughts. Our power within is derived from our ability to think and choose freely. It is therefore imperative to pay attention to the incessant self-talk that circulates within our minds. This internal dialog truly creates the conditions of which we live and evolve. The power we seek does not come from an external source; it comes from within.

- Forgiveness: It is imperative that we don't carry this kind of baggage with us when we exit our earthly bodies. Forgiveness doesn't need to flow in more than one direction. It needs to flow from you to whomever or whatever circumstance you need to heal and forgive. Forgiveness is healing, and it provides freedom to the soul. If you need to make a list of those who have caused you distress by their words or actions and perform a forgiveness ritual, then you should do it. A forgiveness ritual is whatever you need to do to let it go. For example, write it down on paper, send love to the person, and burn the paper—or just think of the person and fill your heart with love and send that love in their direction and let it go, or anything else that is healing that you can think of. If it's possible to let that person know that regardless of how they feel, you've forgiven them and love them, then that's great too. This is a personal, inside job, but to live or die with the burdens of anger or resentment or any other manifestation of fear will do more harm to an individual than whatever you think an individual has done to you.

- Being grateful: Does being grateful bring you happiness? Gratitude is always a tremendously wonderful feeling. It allows us to acknowledge what we have and be thankful for gifts—both big and small. It promotes a view of the glass that is half filled instead of half empty. Gratitude is the one simple emotion that can change a perspective. There are always things to be grateful for, and the more grateful a person is, the more their potential to love expands. Make a list and start counting your blessings!

- Service: Does giving service to others bring you happiness and joy? Create ways to be of service that are meaningful to you—either by the work you do or in your spare time by volunteering. I know there are some boring jobs out there, but if there are other people doing the same boring job, perhaps that's where service begins. It's so nice when others make the workplace brighter with their smiles and laughter. There is always something to be happy about or grateful for . . .

- Absence of unhappiness: Being happy is a decision. Wake up each day and express your love for yourself and the world and make a decision to be happy, regardless of any challenges that come your way. Don't self-anesthetize with substances or drinks that can abuse your system in an attempt to feel better—an overdose of sugar included! As soon as the anesthesia wears off, the challenge that precipitated the action remains, and the cycle will continue until it's interrupted through conscious thought and action. Allow that periodic overdose of sweets to be a once-in-a-blue-moon treat that makes the moment special. Wake up with gratitude and a commitment to yourself to be happy. Make the decision and try to be impervious to the conditions that would sway you away from your goal. There is no magic bullet to get what we want. There is no magic pill that will create a healthy lifestyle complete with good eating and exercise habits, coupled with a positive attitude. There is, however, a choice. A choice to change your mind, change your life, and make it so. Regardless of how awesome other people's lives look from the outside, everyone has their shit. Remember to focus on what your ultimate goal or desire is—not what's in front of you at the immediate moment. Keep your heart and mind on what you really want long term and let that provide the strength to continue. Paste motivational pictures or sentiments around—do whatever is needed to help yourself be your best self.

- Absence of pain: There are wonderful people out there with serious illnesses who live in pain every day. Just to be out of pain would make them feel happy and filled with joy. In this case, it's important for them to work with healthcare providers for pain management and use any integrative therapy to complement conventional wisdom, like energy work or acupuncture. Hopefully, they allow every moment without pain to be a gift that swells self-love. Perhaps they visualize that love, like a precious salve, moisturizing and protecting the body to shield it from pain.

- Contentment: Is it possible to be content with what you have? If not, what do you need? Make a list, check it for realistic properties, and develop a plan to get there. Gratitude helps with contentment. Understanding that within every challenge there is an opportunity, and believing that there is a reason for everything can yield a level of inner peace that fosters contentment.

- Money: I know there are many who think money can buy happiness. If you're wondering, just find somebody who is so wealthy they have more money than they can ever spend who is sick, either mentally or physically, and then ask them. You'll find that a level of income to provide all a person needs and some of what they want can help create the conditions for happiness. Nobody strives to live in hunger or worry about their shelter or safety. Sometimes an individual needs to seek community resources that when coupled with their exemplary work ethic and dedication to diligent effort can create the conditions for them to be happy. Money can be the tapestry to create, but it is of structure and not love. It is a neutral part of a structure that can be used for great things, or it can be used to cheat, be dishonest, or create the conditions for an extensive need for rebalance in our world. Money, if allowed, can be a source of profound discourse among partners, spouses, family members, friends, communities, states, and nations. Money, if allowed, can be a source of innovation, better living, and great hope for a healthier and more harmonious, peaceful earth.

- Being accepted by others and feeling like a part of the group: Is being accepted into partnerships or groups important to your happiness? If that is the case, relationships should be examined closely and honestly. If you feel this is a point of discomfort, look for common denominators. For example, when and where does this lack of acceptance occur? Is it rare, scattered here and there, or is it everywhere? Is it within the confines of a single situation, or has this been a recurring theme in your life? Maybe there's something to consider— people who sacrifice their happiness for others so they'll be accepted know down deep, at some level of consciousness, that they are selling themselves short or selecting the wrong groups to desire inclusion—wrong for them. Perhaps they are trying to fit in where they just don't belong. People who are not accepted because they lack some element of social skill or confidence could benefit from paying attention to the patterns in their lives that dominate the flow. Patterns that occur externally are a result of patterns of thought that reside within the self. These patterns create self-talk that can become like a broken record that just keeps repeating and repeating. Clearing the clutter within should improve the flow of life and resolve some patterns that are no longer in the best interest of an individual. Seeking counsel to understand the triggers that create these feelings or where the source of these feelings is located can be extremely helpful. A person must be ready to step into the shadows created from their negative thoughts. A new group of friends who will love and accept a person for who they are and do not require change would be beneficial, especially if the group encourages growth and self-evolution. One-sided love relationships are also not healthy. Acceptance cannot come at the expense of the self or another person. A person should never compromise their integrity or authenticity to be accepted into any partnership, group, family, or community, regardless of how important that group is to them. In the workplace, when a person feels they don't belong, they need to first evaluate why they feel that way. One needs to contemplate the work group, understand the personalities and intentions of the people, and figure out why they feel like a square peg in a round hole. Is it oversensitivity or lack of self-worth or confidence? Is it because the group vibrates to a frequency that is not consistent with love? Is it because the person does not trust the intentions of the people and needs more time to figure it all out? Or is it because they just don't belong with that organization and that particular group of people? Stick a very positive, optimistic person in a group of Debbie Downers and they won't be able to stand it for long. They certainly wouldn't want to become a Debbie Downer, so they should run away as fast as they can. The opposite is true too—insert a Debbie Downer into a positive, optimistic, highly functioning work team, and they won't be able to stand the vibration of the group—they'll self-select out or somebody will eventually free up their future for the next opportunity if they don't succumb to a better attitude and a more joy-filled existence.

- Doing things for others: Doing things for others can help create the conditions for happiness. It's important, however, to make sure that giving and doing does not happen at the expense of the self. Solid, genuine relationships should be mutually beneficial and encourage people to become the best version of themselves. Relationships take effort to keep working well. It's important that no one individual takes advantage of or abuses another person's kindness or generosity. Sometimes, people do things for others and ignore their own needs because that's where they gain their self-worth and value. There are all kinds of relationships and partnerships out there. Some are unhealthy because they cycle between abuse and forgiveness. It's often difficult to end abusive relationships. There is a wide variety of abuse that occurs in relationships, and abuse can be enveloped in what is perceived as great love and passion. Love, however, is not capable of being abusive. The love for self is intended to protect the body, mind, and spirit, and in doing so, it renders protection to others through the Oneness of being. It's essential to seek professional help if a person feels they are in a codependent relationship that feeds on a cycle of abuse, regardless of the kind of abuse or level of severity. Giving oneself in healthy ways can create conditions for happiness because the activity of giving often feeds the soul and fosters gratitude on many levels. The sacredness of humanity should be acknowledged and respected. Those with a leg up in size, intelligence, financial security, or other positions of strength should never abuse that influence. Being inflated with self-importance is usually a cover-up for insecurities and internal struggles. Remember that love commands the universe.

Opportunities to love and be loved are endless. Loving a pet and helping them to have a beautiful life can also add to a person's happiness meter.

- Empowering or enabling: While we are on the subject of doing things for others, it's sometimes important to ask yourself if your help is empowering or enabling another individual. A parent who solves all their child's problems may make that parent feel good, but it will enable the child and prevent a level of growth, independence, and maturity. A parent who helps the child see the strength, intelligence, wisdom, and resilience within themselves to solve their own problems will empower that child to become a healthy and resilient adult. Resiliency is important in life as it's almost impossible to get through life in one piece without it. Life is filled with challenges and opportunities, and it's essential to see both in any kind of adversity. Sledding down the hill is great fun, but climbing up is what makes it possible. The hard work, step by step, trudging through the snow, using the power of our legs to move, allows for the subsequent relaxation and fun of sledding down a hill, laughter resounding from within. Resiliency comes from learning from mistakes, seeing the silver lining in the gray clouds, and knowing that no matter what, an individual has the internal fortitude to weather any storm.

- Spirituality: It's much better to navigate the challenges of life with an army of love and divinity behind you, on each side and in front, supporting and illuminating the way, than to go it alone. It must be difficult when a person thinks they are alone and must overcome challenges within earthly structure by themselves. The absence of a spiritual connection inhibits a person's realization that they are created from love and supports an unawareness of the divine gifts and resources available to everyone. The pressure of carrying burdens alone can erode the health and well-being of anyone. Knowing that something greater than us exists in any form can make all the difference. Even a connection to the awe and beauty of our universe can create a relationship to spirit. Anything that allows people to know and feel love can aid in creating a spiritual partnership—a partnership that helps people know there is so much more to life than what meets the eye. The idea is to find anything and everything that fosters a feeling of love. For instance, the feeling of love that a person can obtain from a nice deep breath on a warm day with a blue sky and sun shining brightly. We can allow the energy and warmth of sunshine to remind us that we were made from love and that we are love. Love is all we need!

• Our intention should always be to create the conditions for self-love and joy to prosper in our lives. In this state, a natural gravitation toward gratitude, service, and love of all beings and nature will occur. Make a decision to consciously create your day, your week, your life.

Chapter Ten

Cooperating with the Forces of Nature

Life is easier when we go with the flow, as they say. The changes within a journey of hope can be more readily accepted if we have the mindset to cope with the variations in every challenge. As you know, I love to run. Running to me, however, is not just putting one foot in front of the other. I didn't start running until I was fifty-three—the age my mother was when she died. I did it for many reasons, not the least of which was to celebrate being alive and spending time connecting with her while I ran. I am a ChiRunner. In fact, I'm a senior ChiRunning instructor! ChiRunning is a running practice developed by Danny Dwyer, and I shall forever be grateful to him for putting forth a lifetime of love, time, and effort to bring this running technique to the world. The fundamental principles of ChiRunning are energy efficiency and injury prevention. One of the ways we do this is to cooperate with the forces of nature or gravity. We do this in our running form, primarily using a full-foot strike, instead of a heel strike, thereby cooperating with the force of the oncoming road instead of going against it. There are several other nuances, but it's important to have a visual: every time a runner strikes the ground with their heel, they are in a stop and push motion. This is like rolling a square block down a hill instead of a ball. This opposes the force of the road coming the runner's way in the form of gravity and can cause injury. If you get good at cooperating with the forces of gravity, you don't even view a big hill as an exhausting challenge to run up—you merely view it as a necessity to change form. Life is like that too. Opposing the forces of nature has its drawbacks.

I previously addressed these principles of nature—please allow me to summarize once again, because I think they are of utmost importance to recognize. The principle of belief underscores the concept that we create our reality by our thoughts. The mind is a very powerful tool. When the mind works in partnership with love, it maintains the ability to manifest through the power of love and develop hope even in the darkest of times. This partnership of positive thinking and believing, coupled with love-based intentions, has the potential to create the conditions we desire to live in. We all have the ability to make the world a better place, one person at a time, from the inside out. The law of attraction is a concept that gained much attention in recent years and is probably one of the more highly accepted natural beliefs. There are tons of books and articles substantiating the law of attraction. We attract people and situations that harmonize or resonate with our most dominant thoughts or beliefs because energy attracts like energy. You may be saying, "But I thought opposites attract." Opposites attract within the electric fields of magnets; the north (negatively charged) and south (positively charged) poles of magnets located at each end will attract an oppositely charged electric field (moving charges) from a magnetized metal or another magnet. It is a fact to say that the earth is a giant magnet—that's how a compass always knows our north. In many ways, people can be magnets too. Sometimes opposites do attract in life to provide balance to relationships or harmony in situations.

The more we worry about something, the more energy we exude about it and the more life we give it. It's a self-fulfilling prophecy. For instance, during my years at the cancer center, I heard patients say similar phrases to, "I worried about getting cancer so much, I finally got it—I guess I sent that out into the universe too many times." As I became friends with cancer patients through my twenty-three years, I would often get to know them and ask questions about their lives. I've almost done my own tiny study on the cancer patients who would genuinely open up to me, to learn if they were angry or resentful, carried a lot of stress, or had some life-altering experience like the death of a loved one or a divorce that may have precipitated their illness. For some, there was no basis for a cancer diagnosis that could be dreamed up, but for many of them, they carried a lot of stress and baggage. Even with the low percentage of genetic mutations that can cause cancer, there has to be an environmental factor, in addition to the gene, that causes its expression. These environmental factors can be external or internal. I have the Yuka app on my phone. Even though I try, I am surrounded by food, drink, and many other items that can pose a risk to our health—cosmetics, creams, cleaners, and so on. We are bombarded by chemicals, and who can really say how and why they affect some and not others? We had a patient once whom I really loved and became friends with over the years of her treatments. This woman was different from many—no baggage, no bullshit, and a genuinely positive attitude all the time. She was filled with a great deal of light and love, and many gravitated toward her. One day we went to lunch, and I shared my "tiny, made-up study" with her. I told her how she seemed so positive and together, and I asked her if there was any reason she could think of where she might have willed her cancer. I knew she would not be offended as we were real friends. She answered without a second of hesitation, "absolutely." She told me that her son was in an automobile accident, driving in inclement weather after she advised him not to, and he was killed when he was eighteen years old. She told me that she went to the cemetery every day and begged God to die. She told me that the day she wanted to live was the day she got diagnosed with cancer. She chuckled and said, "I was asking for a quick heart attack, not this cancer!" After fighting for five years, they were reunited on the other side. I had another Reiki client and friend who told me that she worked at her family's company and felt overwhelming pressure to work long hours and push herself to limits she really didn't desire. She told me that cancer saved her life because she hated working at that job, and it wasn't until she was sick that she could quit. When she resumed employment after her remission, she went elsewhere, citing that the memories of her disease were too difficult for her to go back to the same place. There is so much we don't really understand, and life is not always what it appears to be!

The principle of concentration that teaches us that whatever we focus on will increase in intensity is most evident for me at night if I can't sleep. Take one little thing that bothers you—or some issue that needs resolution—and in the quiet of the night with a very active and tired brain, new life can be infused into the issue to make a mountain out of a molehill. In the workplace, when any issue gathers more focus, the intensity or necessity of change increases, and with effort a resolution likely comes forth. Love-based thoughts will create more deeply seated, love-based thoughts and will result in the corresponding cascade of human reactions and physiology. These reactions help to create the conditions for a joy-filled life. Fear-based thoughts will create more deeply rooted, fear-based thoughts along with the cascade of human reactions and physiology that correspond to the many faces of fear—manifestations of fear such as fear itself, anger, manipulation, depression, anxiety, control, and so on. These reactions will interrupt the creation of a joy-filled life. The choice is completely individual, but knowing how a human can sabotage themselves with the power of their mind and a lack of love or self-love can be a very helpful tool in building the life one desires. It's also common to ruminate on a challenge or an issue that provokes anger or resentment. The more it's thought about, the larger the issue becomes. Just like a magnifying glass, the more we think about anything, the larger and more focused it becomes—both good and bad, healthy and unhealthy, and so on. It's important when we have negative thoughts that do not serve our highest good that we work diligently on healing them and eliminating them from our constant thoughts. "Let it go" is wonderful advice. Negative thoughts piled up high and deep can cause a person to have a very unhappy life. It can also cause others to not want to be around that negativity. Both negativity and positivity are contagious.

The natural law of substitution can be very helpful. It's the gift whereby it's physiologically impossible for a human to have two opposing thoughts at the exact same time. This gift helps us alter our limiting beliefs and is very helpful when we want to replace feelings and emotions like fear or anger with love. This concept was discussed earlier in the book, but I think it's important to repeat it here. When a person is fearful or angry, they should take a breath and rearrange their thoughts. Thinking of love—of loving and being loved—can alter our internal chemistry at a moment's notice. Once the feeling of love resides within someone's heart, it can be allowed to replace other feelings that need to be banished. Practice makes perfect. I had a friend many years ago who was challenged to replace fear with love. This includes all the many manifestations of fear, especially anger, doubt, and insecurity. I created love exercises for him. Many I have shared this with find it helpful. The ability to recognize fear-based thinking and transition to love-based thinking becomes easier the more you practice and build the shortcuts into your subconscious. Think of it as learning how to drive standard and change gears. At first it's painful, but with time it becomes painless and without thought. So first an exercise to see how they both feel in the body. Sit quietly, eyes closed and think about something that really frosts your keester—something that makes you angry or brings fear. Feel where this emotion is located in your body—a common place is your abdomen/chest area—and let it simmer. Really feel this emotion and pay attention to other parts of your body and take note of how you feel. When you have solidified your awareness of this, start thinking about some person or place that you love. Continue to focus on whatever you've chosen to fill your heart with love. Really feel this emotion and pay attention, once again, to the parts of your body that respond to what you're thinking and feeling. Sit with this feeling and bask in love. I imagine that both exercises elicited very different responses within your mind and body. The more you do this exercise, the more quickly you'll recognize fear-based thoughts. Since it's impossible to have both at the same time, as soon as fear or anger or something negative crops up, switch to the love exercise. Another type of love exercise I developed for some who struggled just to feel love is to sit quietly for five to ten minutes and in your mind, picture people you love. See them smile and laugh, then allow their picture to fade away, only to be replaced by someone else you love. Repeat this as many times as you can, sit still, and when you're done you should be in such a happy place. This is great exercise to reduce stress or get thoughts into a more positive place.

The mind-body principle is the concept whereby every thought has a corresponding reaction in the body, and these impulses are connected by thoughts and memories built on the law of association. Because we become products of our emotions, it's important to know we can control the type of product we become! It's not uncommon for humans to overthink and create problems that don't really exist. The breath of life can be blown into any situation to give it the power to seem real. It creates drama around situations that don't really exist but have been given life through a misunderstanding of some sort. This results in additional and further turmoil or adversity that can drain the joy out of life, especially when the cycle is allowed to repeat over and over . . . the cycle of creating issues that don't really exist. Remember that humans respond to the stimuli of life the way they interpret it—and it's different for everyone. Two people can experience the same situation and react completely differently. In fact, the same person can have the same experience on different days and react very differently. There are mental, physical, emotional, and environmental factors that can influence how we interpret anything. The message is that either love or fear is at the root of all thoughts and emotions. People say they always fear the unknown, but really, they fabricate the elements of the unknown, and that's what makes them so scary. Use your gifts of strength and perseverance coupled with knowing there's an army of angels and other divine beings to help with anything at any time . . . even to find parking spaces or catch an elevator quickly when you're in a hurry and can't find the stairs. Love or fear . . . choose wisely.

Chapter Eleven

Smashing the Pie of Adversity into Smithereens

When problems seem so large that they cause great internal anxiety or struggle, the challenge may be better handled mentally, emotionally, and physically if it is divided into smaller pieces. The smaller pieces will allow a clearer view and less stressful path. It's easier to get through one week than one month. It's easier to get through one day than one week. It's easier to get through one hour than one day. If you are running a marathon, a handy mind game is to break it into segments and conquer the intervals instead of the entire 26.2-mile stretch. I had so much anxiety about running my first marathon, I even dedicated each segment of miles to different people (living or not) for additional motivation. Whatever the overwhelming challenge, it should be sliced into as many smaller segments as it takes for an individual to feel comfortable and less stressed. For some people, writing the plan will work better than thinking about the plan of resolution. The completer and more organized a written plan of resolution is, the easier it will be to follow. The tidier the work area or home, the calmer it will make the people who live there. Clearing clutter encourages more clearing of clutter. This system of thinking works for all types of challenging situations. A person should ask themselves:

- Why am I feeling bad, and what is really bothering me? Do I intuitively feel that this issue resides on the surface, or is it something buried deeper? Do I know the source of this issue and when it started to affect me? Have I worked on elements of this theme before, and am I diving deeper into the meaning and cause? Time and solitude may be needed to contemplate such questions, but be sure to continue to peel that onion skin. As people evolve, over time, an issue may resurface, not because they are taking steps backward but because they are more evolved to go back to that onion and peel deeper layers. Human soul evolution, both individual and aggregate, never takes a step backward—even if people and groups of communities feel that way.

- What elements of each situation do I have control over? For those elements that can be self-controlled through thought and action, identify, plan, and implement the changes. For those elements that rest outside of a person's self-control, identify aspects of the elements that can be thought of differently—a change in perspective to minimize or eliminate the elements of the challenge. Let go of anything that can't be controlled and provides an energy drain with no productive reason or purpose.

- How can I plan a resolution? Don't run away but tackle. Walk into a brighter light, changing directions if necessary. When we walk into the light, the shadow is behind us. Contemplate the path that serves the highest good of all concerned, especially the self. When the self is in order, life is in order.

Contemplate the need for professional assistance. Does this issue reside in my subconscious mind, and do I really have no idea where it's coming from or what I need to do to resolve it? Hypnotherapy may be a great option to consider. The conscious mind asks what the subconscious mind knows.

- Create an affirmation or two. Write them down and say them twice a day for thirty days. You can always hang a copy on your bathroom mirror, behind the bathroom door, or on the inside of a cupboard too!

People are so much stronger than they give themselves credit. Our Creator created humans with all the tools necessary to self-actualize, self-regulate, and self-heal. People have the ability to create the conditions to overcome challenges, learn and grow from them, and feel the divine infrastructure that carries us and illuminates our way. The reason our life plans are co-created is because we are never alone in our decisions, challenges, or celebrations. As an individual overcomes challenges and proves their fortitude to themselves, their resilience will be enriched. Physical exercise can also provide a venue to enrich resilience. Regardless of age, a person can take up some sport, like golf, pickleball, tennis, walking, or running. With time, practice, and proper form, a person can prove their determination and resilience to themselves by accomplishing goals they never thought possible. Make healthy, well-informed, and courageous decisions, and don't look back except to see how far you've come!

Our thoughts and beliefs are often justified to ourselves regardless of how much sense they truly make. It can be easier to step aside and be the observer, acting in the role of stranger. We often go for a haircut or massage and tell those practitioners all our innermost thoughts and feelings. We don't hang out with these people, call them on the phone, or go shopping with them. We see them on varied schedules, yet we pour our guts out to them. Did you ever wonder why? I can think of two reasons—one is we trust them to vent to and get the crap off our chest while they are in a captive situation (like cutting your hair or providing a massage) and can't walk away. The second is that they are not emotionally involved and their advice is often excellent because it is devoid of the toxic details and minutia surrounding the situation. Other than recognizing their names and roles, these service providers or practitioners usually don't know the individuals involved in the discussions. They're also good secret keepers, because honestly, after you leave, they are on to the next client and probably won't remember many of the details of your story. Most importantly, they are not emotionally involved—they are observers. The limitation is they only get one side of the story—although those who are highly intuitive can usually see the reality rests somewhere in the middle of people's perceptions. Fear is not rational, yet it is as real as the nose on your face.

So, practice being the observer. I've told my Reiki clients who couldn't resolve, forgive, or heal a situation to take some alone time and do this weird exercise. Set up two chairs, one writing pad, and one pen. Pour each a glass of water, wine, soda, or anything else that can be enjoyable during this exercise. Sit in one chair and start writing the issues—number them. It's most beneficial if you can list them in the order of importance or severity per your perceptions. When you're done, place the pad and pen in front of the other chair. Now make believe you don't really know yourself or those involved. Relocate to the other chair, take a deep breath, and become the observer. Address each issue with a global, unemotional, or committed view and discuss potential resolutions. Don't move back to the other chair until you've addressed each issue. Speak out loud, just as if there were another person sitting in the opposite chair. Don't stop until you are satisfied that you've received helpful advice from your observing self. Be honest and brave and make sure you tell yourself all the things you don't want to hear but need to hear! If you're worried about a neighbor seeing you through the window, just put a pair of earbuds in each ear. If anyone sees you, they'll just think you're doing what the majority of others are doing, talking on their phones.

Perhaps it would be helpful and hopeful to provide some examples of what I'm talking about, just for greater clarity. First, let's address the clearing of the inside clutter exercise using the bullets that are listed earlier in this chapter. Please note, this is completely fictitious, but I think it's reasonable to say it could happen. The individual in this made-up example states the following:

- I am feeling bad because my coworker had a party and did not invite me. Why does this happen so frequently to me? Why do I so often crave friendships and feel left out of the mix? Why does it bother me so much? I feel like this is not just about how it appears on the surface; I know it triggers something buried deeper, but I'm not sure exactly why I get so upset inside. I don't honestly care that I wasn't invited as I'm not really friends with that group, but what I do care about is the camaraderie I'm never included in. I'm just different from them, I guess. Maybe I'm a jerk. Maybe I'm not fun to be with because I'm introverted and clunky in public. I don't think this goes back to my family as I thought I resolved the issues with my brothers and sisters because I was never included with them either. I was much older. As the oldest child, the next one was born ten years later, with the twins being born two years after. There was no question they loved their older sibling, and as we age we are getting closer, but why is it every time I'm in a situation like this, it makes me angry, resentful, and sad?

- I guess I only have control of myself. I can't make people want to hang out with me. My brothers and sisters are very sporty, and I'm rather heavy, and I didn't want—and actually couldn't—do the things they'd always get together and do. I'm not a skier or a hiker or a runner. Hmmm . . . through this discovery I also feel that I don't like myself. That ten-year age difference and being left out isn't actually what bothers me—it's that I can't do the fun stuff they can because I'm fat. In fact, my size makes me miserable. I don't want to hang out with me—why should anybody else? I'm always apathetic and blah. That's it! Every time I'm excluded it's a reminder that I don't like myself.

- My plan of resolution is that I'm still young and capable and I'm going to fix my physical appearance because I don't feel that great on the inside either. I will not run away but I will tackle this weight and unhealthy living. I'm going to join Weight-Watchers so I'll have others to help motivate and support me. I'm going to join some kind of facility and start exercising. I'm going to start feeling better about myself. I'm going to hang pictures and motivational sentiments around my apartment to remind me that I really want to love myself, and I promise myself that I will become my greatest advocate for change. My siblings love me, and I'll get them to help me too. Regarding the job—I'm just going to look for another one when I'm in a better place and start over. I want more meaning-ful work where I like the work more and feel I could fit in—perhaps a nonprofit that has a noteworthy mission. I'm also going to spend time learning to meditate. I am going to understand myself better, and I know there is an army of invisibles that will help me. I am made from love, and that love is going to get me out of this hole I've dug for my-self. I will feel better within the next six months! If I feel I need professional counseling, I'm going to find a trusting practitioner to seek help, and this time I will not be ashamed or embarrassed.

- My affirmation: I am love. I am strong. I am determined to get healthy and happy. I am grateful. I've got this!

- Perhaps the next example would be of the two chairs, pad, paper, and drink suggestion. Please note, again, that I'm making this up—I'll be writing whatever pops into my head, so it's completely fictitious. This time, the in-dividual in this example states the following:

- Chairs are set up, the pad and paper are on the table, along with two glasses of sparkling cider. I sit quietly thinking of all the crap pissing me off. I get the pad, drink a few sips, and write. In or-der of what's bothering me: (1) I hate my current job; (2) my boyfriend is a jealous, selfish guy, and I'm not happy living in his world; (3) I don't have much money, and living with him saves me a lot each month, but I feel trapped; and (4) my parents can absolutely help, but I've been a shit to them and don't deserve it—they are wonderful, loving people and I have sucked as a daughter.

- I get up, change seats, and speak to the empty chair like they are a stranger or barely an acquaintance, practicing being an observer. This is nice, a fresh glass of sparkling cider for the observer! Observer me responds to each element on the list:

  ° Life is too short to begin with, let alone having a job you don't like. You have to make a change. There's a saying that goes, if you really love what you do, you don't work a day in your life. Of course that's an oversimplification, since nobody loves the challenges of their job every day, but hopefully you understand the sentiment. You need to either change jobs as quickly as you can or change your mind about the job and stop letting it zap the life out of you. Those really are the only two choices here—change your job or your mind. I ask my non-observer self if there are reasons for this job that are ultimately in their best interest. For example, perhaps it offers great experience for your résumé or it's a great means to an end because it provides a good income to temporarily assist you with furthering your education or allowing you time to reevaluate. It's going to take confidence, resilience, and perseverance to figure this out, but you were created with every tool you need in-side yourself—and besides, there's a reason for everything. If you don't know what you want to do next, change your mind about the job and find something meaningful to fill your soul in the meantime, such as volunteering with dogs.

° Relationships are not easy, and each one pro-vides a great purpose in life for some reason that you may or may not be aware of. People can alter their behavior, but never expect or wait for somebody to change. You are complaining about fundamental personality traits that have likely been seeded since your boyfriend was a child. His personality may work for some, but your concerns sound like red flags that indicate he's not the right person for you. You should se-riously consider a breakup. Living with him does not appear to be within your highest good, and money and fear should never be your drivers. Put more effort into being a giver instead of a taker—you gather that which resonates with your most dominant thoughts and actions. It's not easy to stand up for yourself and move on, but looking back, I bet you'll be happy you did.

° Your parents sound like they are loving people. Loving parents love their children through thick and thin, and I'm sure your actions may have confused or disappointed them in the past, but that love—that bond of parent and child—runs far deeper than you think. You should contact them and ask for nothing but their love and for-giveness. It won't take much time if you are sincere in your efforts to be able to be honest with them, confide in them, and ask for their help. Although you feel you don't deserve their help, just sharing that with them will help you to forgive yourself. They will welcome you back in their lives because when push comes to shove, there's nothing that can compare with the love a parent has of their children *(Mare's addition— not within this paragraph—this is assuming the parents are not dysfunctional and there's no other factors at play, since this whole situation is make-believe and I'm just typing away here pretending.)* Don't let your ego get the best of you. Go home, apologize, do better, and get your life together. Allow their love to be the pillar that keeps you upright during this process.

Hopefully these made-up examples give you some idea of what I'm talking about. The challenges and resolutions can be anything, but know that somewhere inside you are all the answers you seek. These exercises are all about infusing light into darkness and transforming despair into hope. Love yourself enough to be an honest observer who doesn't tell you what you want to hear but tells you what you need to hear.

Chapter Twelve

Co-creation and the Plan of Hope

Part of understanding life and accepting its challenges includes an understanding of how we got to planet earth and why things are not always what they appear. The more aware we are of our soul-time before and after birth, the better we understand the reasons or purpose of challenge. In chapter 3, the co-created plan was briefly described, but it's important to truly understand this phenomenon because our lives depend on it. Often, circumstances in our lives are so bewildering that we cannot fathom the reason for such conditions, and we certainly would not expect ourselves to have had anything to do with creating such heartbreaking, difficult, or tragic situations. Therefore, trusting yourself is the first step in the acceptance and understanding of difficult circumstances and the creation of hope. It's paramount to trust that before we landed on earth, our soul and divine council knew exactly what was best for us—the elements of life that would serve our highest good and be consistent with our life's purpose to reach the level of soul evolution we set out to achieve. Everyone has been created by and from love. Using love to navigate the blueprint we set before us to evolve to the highest level of consciousness that is individually possible and vibrate to the highest corresponding vibration is our ultimate goal. At the end of our lives, we are allowed a review, given all the data points and lifetimes along the way. We can examine the goals we attained and those where we missed the mark. We can choose to reincarnate in years, decades, or centuries—or we can do the work on the other side and evolve there. Our plans are often indelibly intertwined with other people's co-created plans, and our soul groups come to earth in agreement to serve each other's highest good. Serving the highest good, however, doesn't always feel good. It is through adversity that we become resilient and strong. It is through adversity that we become creative to develop a route to more peaceful grounds. It is through adversity that we begin to know the God within us and develop pride in what we have overcome and rallied through. It is through adversity that we celebrate our authentic self that never wavers in love and truth.

If we accept that everyone has a co-created plan that was created with their highest good in mind, then we understand that our role is to trust and accept both our own plans and others. These are the keys to a more joyful and hope-filled life. The parent who loses a child experiences the worst grief possible. A grief so suffocating that the future temporarily lacks any kind of luster or hope. Why anyone would put something like that in their co-created plan seems unconscionable. From anyone's perspective, losing a child of any age does not make sense, let alone accepting that an individual would plan that tragic path within their life's journey. Our earthly view is one of pain, sadness, heartbreak, and loss without reason. If we reach outside ourselves to our heavenly view, we can try to fathom possibilities or examples of why a child would put that in their plan and why any parent would agree.

To gain any semblance of clarity, let's think of a few totally hypothetical and completely fictional possibilities.

Example one: In another lifetime, the parents could have been rulers who created the conditions for starvation and death for a family among the village. To balance this karmic tragedy, the one who suffered agrees to be born to these parents, but only for a short time. Perhaps they elect to come to earth as an angelic soul because they are already highly evolved, due to the adversity of their precious lifetimes, but they lovingly agree to play this role for the repenting rulers. These rulers come to earth as husband and wife to experience the greatest loss and most heartfelt tragedy they can create for themselves. The parents use their grief, however, to create something special on earth, in honor of their child, which will leave precious imprints within the fabric of time and will surely make the world a better place than they found it. The three souls have allowed the universe to rebalance the original unfairness and maltreatment under the direction of the plan created by themselves. Example two: Two souls that have incarnated together many times in the past, having various roles in each other's life as men or women, create a life plan subsequent to a review of current and past lifetimes. They clearly understand that one of their past life shortcomings, continually repeated throughout lifetimes, was a sense of apathy. They realized that their plan needed to include some life-altering event that would instill a higher level of tenderness and render a more compassionate and empathetic outlook on life. In conjunction with their divine counsel, they created a plan that would include the loss of a precious child. The soul that agreed to be their offspring was highly evolved and knew that the mark they would make on those they met, although it would be for a short time, would be extremely valuable to many, as would the loss. There are so many stories we can make up to explain this situation, but the take-home message is that there is a reason. We may not know the reason until our death and earthly review, but what's important is that we trust ourselves and accept that life is almost always not what it appears to be.

I write this with conviction because of what I've learned from my own guides, the angelic realm, saints, prophets, and avatars that communicate with me, but almost more important are the experiences I witnessed myself in my many years of providing heart-centered hypnotherapy. Almost eight out of ten clients went to another lifetime to resolve their current issue(s). The first time a hypnotherapy client went to another lifetime was during my training, before I became certified. At that time, I recall being surprised and wondered if it was really true, but as my practice developed, there were so many who regressed to a previous lives, with incredible consistencies among all of them, that there was no question in my mind that these clients were accessing previous lives. Why the universe sent me so many who traveled back in time to other lifetimes eluded me, but I trusted there was a reason. In each session, I was astounded by how I knew what to say and do to help my clients achieve remarkable healing, but within a short time I realized, once again, I was merely a conduit that could take direction from a divine infrastructure of resources that were not visible to the naked eye. I gained perspectives and understanding of previous lives that I would never have acquired without them. I knew that for whatever reason, the universe was sending me those clients who needed a past life regression to heal an issue occurring in their life. With regression we can often access our Akashic Records. This can be a transformative experience when it allows for the exploration of our history of thoughts and actions throughout the life of the soul. The Akashic field of energy can provide clarity and healing from those situations in life that we can't seem to resolve from a lack of understanding. These meditations or regressions allow us to access the wisdom of our soul and can offer incredible insights into limiting or sabotaging patterns that continue to hound us. The Akash can also provide a path of understanding of our purpose in this lifetime and future paths that may present at any time. The records allow us to gain insights that align with our higher self and what is truly in our best or highest interest.

Interesting story as an aside, when I was in my mid-twenties I was on an airplane going to a clinical microbiology and immunology symposium in California. I sat next to a nice-looking gentleman but did not speak to him during the flight as I was reading a book, the title of which I don't recall. As we walked off the plane, the gentleman asked me if I had ever read Dr. Brian Weiss's book, *Many Lives, Many Masters*. I replied no. He then told me that someday that book would be very important to me, and then we said goodbye and have a nice trip. I never saw him again. Over twenty-five years later, I met Dr. Brian Weiss and attended a five-day intensive workshop on past life regressions. I was drawn to that conference and training because so many of my clients traveled to past lives to resolve current issues, and I wanted to make sure I deeply understood various techniques and meanings from the expert of all experts. Brian Weiss, MD is an extraordinary and loving man and physician who has written a plethora of books on reincarnation, life plans, the resolution of past wounds, and the alignment of future challenges in future lifetimes, when issues repeat because they have not been healed, such as addictions or anger and hate issues. I highly recommend any of his books. I learned a lot in that one week, and it's my experiences through the years that inspire me to share what I have gathered from others. I love this Facebook post by Dr. Weiss:

> Love is an absolute and eternal energy. It is our Source. This explains the remarkable consistency of messages received from departed loved ones, whether in regressions, dreams or directly. "Do not grieve so much for me, I am still here, I am always with you, and I will love you forever." And we are constantly being reunited with our loved ones, either on the other side or back here, once again in physical bodies.

Sometimes I think of that gentleman on the plane knowing that his comment was extraordinary and provided by spirit. I wish I could say thank you to him for his incredible insights into the far future—he was gifted to say the least.

Most agree that the Bible does not teach reincarnation. The Christian faith supports a single, earthly lifetime followed by death, judgment, and soul deposition to whatever level of eternal destiny is deserved from that lifetime—namely heaven, hell, or purgatory. Reincarnation, however, is a central belief in many Eastern religions, including Hinduism, Buddhism, Sikhism, and Jainism. There are also mystical religions that include beliefs in reincarnation.

I can remember being on the fence in my mid-thirties about reincarnation. I was still very Catholic, saying the rosary daily, and getting through shit days at work by relating to the first sorrowful mystery, Agony in the Garden. That structure of belief is what I needed at that time. As my self-mastery journey progressed, however, and I became more exposed to other religions and historical facts about the Roman Empire and the formation of the early Christianity and the Roman Catholic Church, I began to sincerely and seriously contemplate the existence of reincarnation. It just didn't make sense to me that we only get one shot at planet earth. If I had doubts, spending ten years with a busy practice of Reiki and hypnotherapy sealed that deal. There is no question in my mind that re-incarnation not only exists, but it's also one of the greatest options we have been blessed to receive. Since there is a reason for everything, perhaps that's why 95 percent of my clients solved current issues with past life regressions. I often need proof—and I sure received a lot of it.

I would imagine a religion with a dogma that excludes reincarnation greatly benefits the structure, as it only gives a person one chance to get it right, thereby exerting incon-spicuous and subtle control. Eternal damnation is some-thing to fear even for a short stint, let alone an eternity.

During my hypnotherapy sessions, some issues that my clients released and healed included but were not limited to food or drug addictions, sexual misconduct or abuse, poor relationships, feelings of unworthiness, and consis-tent self-sabotage. During every session I knew I was di-rected by the spirit world to proceed in the manner I did and speak the words I spoke. I felt it was remarkable to be guided through a client's hypnotherapy session. I un-derstood that my role was to be a conduit to this type of healing. I am a certified heart-centered hypnotherapist through The Wellness Institute (wellness-institute.org), and our role is to assist people in healing themselves by releasing current or past life patterns that interfere with the love-filled life we are meant to live.

The continual development of our personal and pro-fessional journey of hope operates independently in the background of our lives, guiding our attitudes and per-ceptions of the world around us, affecting our conscious decisions and outlooks on life. What I mean is it's not likely we sit and contemplate, examine, or study our journey of hope—it's innately created as we go along. It can, how-ever, be helpful to give this journey some thought as we contemplate the challenges we endure and the reactions we exhibit to overcome or deal with them. This journey of hope develops from a voluminous amount of experience and feedback through lifetimes and can assist us in mak-ing conscious decisions. This journey of hope becomes part of the alignment of our physical, mental, emotional, and spiritual lives if we trust ourselves and accept a few caveats of earthly life. Even if we live to be one hundred years old, it's a drop in the ocean of soul life. Although there is no time back home, we have existed for what we would humanly view as millennia.

To review, before we are born, we develop a plan for our earthly life. We do this in conjunction with a divine in-frastructure; therefore, it's co-created. We are the primary authors of this plan, but there is a divine network that will guide, nurture, assist, motivate, and provide strength and courage to us as we journey through life. They will nudge us if we fall outside of the plan and provide intuitive mes-sages or signs to assist with our decision-making. We will not feel the alignment of mind, body, and spirit if we ig-nore the internal navigation systems we were blessed to have access to in our lives. Pay attention to discomfort and to any intuitive nudging by the self. There is a part of all of us that maintains the wisdom of the world. If we are fortunate and it's in our plan, our relationship with this divine network will be known to us—or at least parts will be known to us, and we will be able to communicate with that council. We incarnate with a soul family who mutually agrees to assist each other in all journeys. We put ele-ments in our path as reminders. We include features of the plan that we hope pops out during life to help us make decisions and stay on path. To stay on the path, it's helpful to listen to our hearts and higher selves and keep our egos in check. We usually know when we are in the right place doing what we hoped because it feels good and right, and we know when we are not in a place consistent with our highest good or our co-created plan because it doesn't feel good or right. The key is to be able to inquire within and check in regarding your alignment—alignment of your physical, mental, emotional, and spiritual presentation. We can feel alignment, and the next chapter will provide greater insights into this gift. When we live a life that is fundamentally consistent with the path we outlined for ourselves before birth, we stay in alignment, even when life throws us incredible challenge. We may be amid incredible challenges or grief, but we still have an intuitive knowing that we remain in alignment.

Our co-created plan is developed amid full disclosure and a complete dataset of all other lifetimes. As I said, when we die, we do a life review. We examine those aspects of our plan that we accomplished and those we failed to recognize and bring to fruition. We evaluate the resolution of issues we intended to complete, whether these aspects of healing involved ourselves or included others. When we make plans to reincarnate, we update our plan. We look at the aspects of the self that need additional healing or spiritual growth, and we therefore include opportunities to reach those goals. We know that reaching those goals is not always a walk in the park. In fact, we grow so much more through adversity than we do during our celebrations and easy times. We work out karma between and among loved ones, family, friends, and enemies.

Through mutual agreement, we select our parents and siblings. It is highly likely that we have lived other lives with these people in various capacities. Each have been men and women, mothers, fathers, spouses, siblings, friends, acquaintances, etc. The delegation changes with the goals and objectives that exist in mutual plans and any unresolved karma or issues. For example, two people develop a plan that includes marriage that may or may not end in divorce, but the marriage was needed to complete some life issue or karmic connection. The children that agree to be born of these parents know the marriage may result in divorce and accept that plan, as divorce may instill some characteristics or challenges they need to evolve in their plan. Nothing is happenstance. We are on a trajectory that offers opportunities for greater love and compassion. The end game is to vibrate to the highest frequency possible—in the love and light of all that is.

Chapter Thirteen

Physical, Mental, Emotional, and Spiritual Alignment

A person has the ability to experience and identify physical, emotional, mental, and spiritual alignment. Alignment is an innate gift that acts like a navigation, support, alert, and early warning and detection system. It is connected to everyone's innate, divine wisdom as well as the collective wisdom of the collective consciousness. It is powered by love. Alignment in this context is a perception, feeling, or intuition that communicates information to its owner.

Meditation or just sitting in stillness are ways to experience and assess alignment, and it can become an excellent teacher to help develop skills of discernment. Once an individual is tuned into evaluating their various states of alignment, changes can be more easily detected and acted upon. Depending on the issue, with practice, a person can tune into their alignment system and gather information about what's going on inside in seconds. Other times, with more complex issues, the alert can act like a slow burn that works diligently to get your attention.

A lack of alignment is a feeling of discomfort when a person knows that something is not right. The location where these feelings manifest can differ with different people or situations. Commonly, a person may feel a sense of discomfort in their chest area—or some place along the invisible, vertical axis that splits the body in half from the top of the crown to the pelvic area. It could be uneasiness in the stomach area, chest, neck or throat, etc. It's highly recommended for an individual to get in touch with this system and learn how to interpret its messages. With practice, a human can understand how to decipher messages from this innate wisdom. This is not some special power that only some have, it is an internal power that is accessible to everyone who makes an effort to recognize and understand it. When we continue to ignore the signals from our internal alignment system, a divine part of us works diligently to get our attention, using whatever methods are necessary to do so, always in the spirit of what is in our highest good. Our higher self may do whatever it needs to garner our attention, including immersing our physical, mental, or emotional bodies into levels of discomfort that can appear debilitating. This early warning system, if left unattended, can develop into some kind of illness or disease. Some will point out that dis-ease is a state of being that develops from the inside out. Since we manifest situations that resonate with our dominant thoughts, it's not uncommon for an illness to present as an unintentional savior from something we need an excuse to eliminate from our lives. To be clear, we can never feel guilty that we caused some illness or disease intentionally or unintentionally to happen to ourselves or others, but when we acknowledge that our co-created plans include all kinds of speed bumps—some that may even be terminal—we must accept that there is a reason and that we agreed to accept the challenge for whatever we delineated to be within the ultimate highest good for our soul's growth and spiritual evolution with the objective to obtain the most precious and infinite supply of pure, divine love. We have developed soul agreements or contracts with many individuals who we placed in our path for a purpose. That purpose does not always manifest as joy and elation. Every relationship has value—even those fleeting acquaintances as well as those who have been genuine thorns in our sides. Regardless of how long a relationship lasts, it can be purposeful enough for us to acknowledge its value.

I've included an exercise to assist you in discovering the nuances of this alignment system. To start, think of a situation that was clearly not good for you, some circumstance or event that was not in your best interest and highest good. Perhaps this less-than-optimal situation was a difficult or dysfunctional former relationship; perhaps you felt manipulated by a partner, friend, or employer; maybe it was a negative living arrangement that caused great pressure or stress; perhaps it was excessive stress or pressure you placed upon yourself; or maybe an individual was trying to influence or control you to do something you didn't want to do. It could have even been a situation when you were doing something or eating something unhealthy for your body, you knew it was not in your best interest, and it caused you great discomfort. Sometimes a lack of alignment can affect others too. States of alignment affect our attitudes and moods. Negativity is contagious, so it's not unusual to exude negative energy and have it affect others. When you have selected your thoughts to focus upon for this exercise, hold on to them and continue with the exercise.

Sit quietly, clear your mind as best as you can and breathe deeply, inhaling and exhaling to totally relax the body. When you feel relaxed, pretend that situation is happening again . . . really pretend and relive it. Allow the feeling of discomfort to develop and expand within. When it's palpable, take note of where the discomfort is located in your body. If you had to give it a color, what would the color be? Explore all the connections between the situation and your body. Pay attention to the smallest details of where in your body you can feel the discomfort manifest and linger. When you've noted all this, bring love to the situation, heal it, and let it go. This is similar to the exercise we discussed earlier in this book to prove that physiologically we cannot have love and fear occupy the same space at the same exact time. Fill your heart with love and light until all the discomfort has been eliminated, and then evaluate what happened. Take notes if it's helpful. Really understand that exercise.

We can learn meaningful shortcuts for immediate awareness the next time similar feelings of discomfort develop. Do this simple exercise with various situations that have occurred that bothered you so you can feel the different places in your body that are affected by different types of adversity or negativity. Try to develop an internal measurement and alert system that can help you make decisions and select good choices for your future. Perfect this system and not only will it let you know when you should or should not do something—it can become an early warning and detection system that runs automatically in the background, like antivirus software that can alert you immediately when something is not optimal. Alignment and intuition are indelibly intertwined. It's like intuition tunes into a higher power and signals the internal alignment system to communicate rapidly via feelings or emotions in the body. Sometimes a person will not understand why something inside feels out of alignment, but they'll know something is up because they feel "crooked." If this is ever felt, take a few moments to relax and breathe deeply and start asking yourself questions. With time and practice, you will be able to pinpoint the source of what's bothering you quickly and accurately. The first step in resolution is identifying the existence of an issue so a plan can be developed to realign.

A lack of alignment occurs when a person is not giving their body what it needs. Alignment can be associated with the physical body if your higher self understands that it would be the fastest way to get your attention. For instance, eat crap for a while and your body will feel like crap. If an extremely healthy eater eats poorly for a few days, their physical and mental alignment will be out of whack because it's not consistent with the patterns they've established for themselves. How about the person who eats poorly all the time and the sludge within the body begins to feel normal? Eventually there will be issues—chronic exhaustion, diabetes, high cholesterol, high blood pressure, thyroid issues, gastrointestinal issues, and so on. Sometimes these issues are a result of genetics, and sometimes they are purely a result of life choices. Even genetic predispositions often need some other environmental force to activate an issue. These forces can be associated with physical exposure or factors affecting a person's mental health and mood. It's difficult to live with an individual who doesn't take stock in their well-being. We were given a precious and miraculous gift called the human body. We should pay attention to everything we purposefully put into our mouths and breathe into our lungs.

The same alignment detection and alert system will activate upon sleep deprivation or incessant negative self-talk. If a person continues to tell themselves they suck, the belief system associated with this negative assessment can have harmful effects on the mind, body, and spirit. It's important to pay attention to every feeling or sense of yuck—like something is just not right. Another example would be a person who loves somebody who is upset because some negative interaction caused a perceived separation in their relationship or friendship, causing a void that feels bad. It begins as a subtle alignment issue, and it continues to fester until that discomfort is like an ache that won't go away until the situation is addressed. Let's say it reaches a point where the individual realizes it's necessary to reach out to the other person, mend fences, and forgive the whole situation to restore their alignment. The relief can be similar to venting, like when there's an issue and you spew what's bothering you and you subsequently feel like a ton of bricks have fallen off your shoulders. There is potential that even with dialog and one-sided forgiveness, the other person will want nothing to do with their former friend or acquaintance and decide to totally cut off the relationship and any further contact. Since the only person a person can control is themselves, each individual will have to rely on their resilience, accept the new form of the relationship, and accept the other person's wishes by letting the internal struggle pass. What is most important is to forgive and move on because that's always in an individual's best interest. One-way forgiveness is liberating and healthy, regardless of its level of reciprocation. Alignment is restored when a person takes care of themselves. Discomfort speaks volumes and is a great tool to alert the body that some element needs attention. As the self-mastery journey continues, this tool becomes perfected.

A person can use this tool to get themselves back on track. When a person is out of alignment they can acknowledge and accept what the alert system is telling them and create a plan of resolution. Resolution doesn't need to take place immediately, but a sincere plan will usually allow the system to ease and give an individual time to resolve without discomfort. It's similar to the concept that the first step in change is acknowledging that one is needed. The knowing and realization can be freeing. In any situation that causes distress or misalignment, only two choices exist to resolve it: change the situation or change your mind about it. Another example: a person may feel their job is not satisfying and be miserable every day. This may be the catalyst to further their education and change careers so they can gain a new outlook and become excited about their new future. The excitement about their new future can neutralize current negative thoughts. A person should not waste precious energy allowing negativity to fester and spread. Negatively has no value except to erode the health and well-being of the person who is thinking negatively. It also sets up a dominant thought pattern that can attract situations that most closely resonate with it—thereby creating more challenge or additional opportunities for negativity. A change in perspective will be necessary to nullify the negative potential. More positive thoughts should bring a person back into alignment, or at least better alignment. A person always has the ability to choose how they think. There is always a choice.

Mental or emotional alignment issues are commonly associated with human relationships. A person can accept or forgive another person or situation to alleviate their mental and emotional discomfort. They can free themselves from the misalignment by ending a bad relationship. A person can respond to misalignment if they're living with someone or people who don't serve their highest good by making a plan to move elsewhere; this includes their current state, city, town, or village. Individuals can always seek professional help to gain clarity and courage to make a change.

Spiritual alignment feels really good inside, as it's a knowing that we are never alone and we are always loved and protected. It lets a person know that what they believe and practice resonates from deep within, and they are on a spiritual path that is fulfilling their spiritual desires and soul growth. When there is spiritual misalignment, there can be a feeling of emptiness, a longing for a divine truth, or a relationship with our Creator who loves us beyond comprehension. If a person follows what resonates inside, it will lead to the right path, and when on the right path, alignment feels splendid.

Perhaps a person can't sleep at night. A lack of alignment often affects sleep. Perhaps it's from lamenting about the past—something that time can't erase and all the grief a person can muster won't change. That's when it's time to let it go—find some way to forgive the past, heal the wounds, and move on. Maybe it's writing in a journal to let your innermost confidential feelings out from where they are trapped. Maybe it's a letter that is written to a person but never given to them. Maybe the letter is burned, and as the paper dissolves into the air, so do the trapped feelings of hurt. When any level of healing is accomplished, alignment in that area will begin to be restored, and an individual will know they are healing themselves. Perhaps it's from worrying about the future. Worry is one of those activities that consume great resources for little return. The best way to set worry free is for the person to have faith that they have the trust and resilience to walk through any challenge, and they have the ability to accept anyone's co-created plan. Knowing each of us has access to an army of angels that are ever ready to protect, support, and guide also helps set worry free. It's ideal to keep yourself in the present moment as much as possible. Being present can provide many rewards—it can maintain a sense of love, purpose, resilience, gratitude, and alignment. Gratitude and alignment also walk hand and hand. It's a fact that sometimes a person has to be present to win!

Alignment can also be viewed as a tool to evaluate balance in a person's life. Work/life balance is important to maintain alignment. When we are off balance, our alignment system kicks in via some form of discomfort to give us a wake-up call of some sort. Discomfort is one of the greatest gifts our minds and bodies give us, for it is invaluable in helping us continuously evaluate the choices we make and the paths we travel in life. From the feeling of impending danger when our hair begins to stand on end, to that gnawing feeling in the pit of our stomachs, to the muscle pain in our necks, to the tightness and ache in our jaws, to the anxiety that mimics chest pain, to the gastric ulcer that forms from ongoing stress, to diarrhea, to headaches, to the pain and suffering of emotional challenges, to dis-ease, the body uses various mechanisms to get our attention and let us know something is not quite what it should be in our lives. There is incredible value in paying attention to the various levels of discomfort in our lives because it often parallels the alignment of our journey with our highest good.

I used my internal alignment system in my career frequently. When a project was being proposed or some strategic initiative or plan was being contemplated, I always took a moment to check into this divine internal navigation system. When my desires were for the good of the whole (I didn't function any other way), I could tap into my alignment to see if all systems were go—or if this project was not in the best interest of the whole (me included). When some idea or proposal was too complicated or convoluted or the risks overrode the potential rewards, I could feel that communication within myself. The internal sign I most often received when something was not aligned to the highest good of all was nausea. At the other end of the spectrum, when a plan was going to work well or significantly assist in the improvement of the lives of others, I could feel my heart wanting to explode with love and excitement. Now that I'm retired, I'm going to admit that this internal system was never wrong. In the end—perhaps after my due diligence—I would always know how to proceed. And this system also could alert me to people who did not possess the values or intentions that were conducive to the work environment or level of integrity I mandated for myself and others. Using this intuition or alignment system in my career definitely added to any success my teams and I ever achieved. When it comes to a human's five senses, having a sixth is always an advantage. We all have access to that sixth sense, but sadly many either don't acknowledge its presence or think it's silly. I can now say I have a track record that proves it's indispensable.

Discomfort is an innate gift, not a burden or sacrifice or duty. There is no martyrdom in possessing discomfort. Self-mastery cannot be fully expressed by putting forth effort to expand our consciousness and develop our intuition while we neglect our physical health and well-being. We have chosen to come to earth with these precious vessels we call our bodies. Our bodies deserve and need attention and care. Our physical bodies and our breath are what differentiate our realm of existence from humanness to spirit. The self-mastery journey, therefore, has a physical component that mandates a general awareness and education. It is vital to understand how our thoughts affect our emotions and feelings in our bodies. It's also imperative to understand all the factors that cause a cascade of internal reactions that affect our health and well-being.

Remember, we react to any stimuli from our own, individual point of reference. We are products of our environment. We all need the sun and the rain to grow and be nourished. We never know the percentage of sun (love) or rain (challenge) that has provided the fundamental building blocks of other people's personalities. When somebody's life experiences a significantly greater magnitude of rain, they can develop in one of two ways. They can become compassionate, driven, tolerant, and resilient, or they can become victims. These victims may maintain nasty dispositions, thinking that life has dealt them a bad hand of cards and nothing is their fault. Things are not always what they appear to be. Discomfort should be like a bell that rings in your head and says, "Hey! Pay attention! Something is not right." It's a given in life that we usually have at least one piece of the puzzle that is missing or doesn't fit properly—but it's important to understand what we can control and what we can't. It is in loving that we are loved, it is in forgiving that we are forgiven.

Chapter Fourteen

In Memoriam: Yesterday

While it is nothing you don't already know, healing from loss is a very difficult journey, especially when it comes to loved ones—and that includes our furry friends and pets. I love my dogs so much that my heart hurts when I think about losing them. Their lives are so precious, their love unconditional, and regardless of how long they live, it's not long enough. The loss of parents, partners, children, and friends can seem overwhelming and hardly bearable. Having the resilience to cope comes with the ability to view loss differently. That doesn't mean it won't be wrought with pain, it only means we will find a way to climb out of the sadness and continue to live with peace and joy for them as we acknowledge and believe they are free to fly in the sea of ultimate love. A dull ache may exist for many years, but the hope is that one day sadness will be replaced with joy and gratitude for the life we were allowed to accompany them on.

The thing about loss to remember, that I believe helps us learn to live with the void that can never be replaced and just learned to live with, is that we experience loss every day. I know it's cliché to say that we only have today or there's only the present, but as time ticks forward, we never get that previous second back. When my girls were little, I would sit and stare at them, knowing that their infancy and youth were short and time would pass quickly. I used to tell myself to burn the memory of these moments into my brain so I'd never forget them—what the girls looked like and what those babies smelled like and how they discovered new things daily. Sadly, regardless of how hard we try, years take clarity out of those photos of the mind, and each year the resolution becomes less clear and vibrant. I look at physical pictures that captured the moments, but the details fade as time marches forward. As our children grow, we often lament about how fast the time flew—it's the same with anything we love. No matter how much we acknowledge the preciousness of the moment, the moments pass, and we continually deal with loss. We deal with loss every second of every day. Some levels of loss are more significant than others, but nonetheless it is loss.

As I'm writing this book, we lost my daughter's precious pup Rosie. Rosie was a ginger-colored miniature poodle who lived only ten years and died peacefully with my daughter and son-in-law by her side, taking her last breath from congestive heart failure naturally, surrounded by their love. Rosie was my first grand pup—she was the initiator of the name Mimi, as when my daughter got her, she told me it was time to decide on a name for me that would carry to all grand dogs and grandchildren. Words can't express how much I loved and still love Rosie. When Rosie was two years old, I'd be so sad after she spent a weekend with me and returned home to my daughter that I had to get my own miniature poodle to fill that void—enter Millie the Dog—who is a famous author now!

As I watch Rosie videos, my heart is so happy for the time we had together, but the sadness of how much I miss her is real. This sadness never goes away—I will miss her hugs and licks forever. Sadness does become more bear-able with time, however, as we become accustomed to living with loss. In addition, I can feel Rosie when she's around, and sometimes at night I can feel her and when I put my hand there to see if it's Millie who is moving, but there is nothing there. Those feelings help heal loss because the loss is only of a physical presence. The soul remains very active. I had a disagreement with a Roman Catholic priest once. I loved him and we often met for lunch. He was adamant that dogs and other animals didn't have souls. He said only humans have that God-given gift. I am positive—100 percent certain—that every living thing that you can communicate with on the other side is due to their loving soul—pets included. I know Charlie, my green-cheeked conure I had for eighteen years, hangs around me. I kiss his urn every time I dust!

Non-dog or pet people probably think people who think like me are crazy, but those who really love animals will admit the pain is just as real as the loss of any hu-man we love. The pain of losing my mom fifty-two years ago was replaced by sheer love and gratitude many years ago. After her death, each year, I'd relive each moment from the time my uncle called my dad at four o'clock in the morning and I reached the phone in the kitchen faster than he reached the phone by his bedside. I heard the discussion and was devastated. Devastated but prepared. Prepared by my mother who promised she'd always be by my side and never leave me. I knew she was telling the truth and from four o'clock in the morning on November 16, 1973, I could feel and hear her. The process of heal-ing was absolutely facilitated by feeling her presence and being able to communicate with her. I know Rosie is in the same place—I feel her presence often, and I know the

newness of sadness will get better with time and acceptance. As life goes on, I am profoundly aware that there
will always be more loss. Loss of the moments, as well as
the loss of dear friends and loved ones. Like my dad would
tell me when he was in his nineties, "If you want to live a
long time, you deal with losing so many people you love."

When we acknowledge that loss occurs every day, and
somehow we manage to cope, we recognize that we have
everything we need inside of ourselves to cope with loss.
When we recognize that the soul lives on—pets included—and that we will see all those we loved when we get
to the other side, we acknowledge that death and loss
does not exist. When we get to the other side, we realize
that time is a human conception to bring structure and
organization to our lives.

Time is a spiral of events that are forever captured in
the ethers or Akash to be accessed whenever we want.
What does this mean? It means that when we are in spirit
form, we can go back to the vibration of anything that occurred within the fabric of our humanly created time and
be there once again. We can be a fly on the wall, or we
can assume the role we played as if in a dream to be there
once again. On the other side places can also be recreated
to lend familiarity and joy. There is no loss. Although we
die and bring nothing with us except our vibration of love
that has been nurtured by the sum total of all our lifetimes
of deeds, we have everything we need and want. We are
known by that vibration, like the physical and unique fin-
gerprint that identifies us while in the flesh. We can create
or recreate whatever continues to feed our souls and pro-
pel our vibration of love.

Chapter Fifteen

Weeds of Consciousness

We are immersed in distraction and drama. The world stage is filled with deception and confusion, and many people have no clue which seat in the theater they can select to see and hear the truth. Discernment and connection to spirit is imperative during these times of clutter and corruption. Our internal and external challenges should be triggers to wake up and make choices for ourselves. The weeds of consciousness grow fast and fastidiously.

Earlier in this book, I mentioned various levels of consciousness, and I'd like to explore them in more detail. Let's start with the most common with which you are likely the most familiar. The first level of consciousness we will consider is called conscious awareness. Conscious awareness includes history, events, situations, facts, and knowledge or wisdom from experiences that an individual can access readily and recall immediately or with contemplation. Conscious awareness is the state where we know things off the top of our heads or access them within our memories. You are in a state of conscious awareness as you read this, and I'm hoping you're reaching outside of your comfort zone to open your mind to new possibilities. As I said before, we go through different levels of conscious awareness several times throughout the day—from fully aware to daydreaming to dreaming while asleep.

Next level to explore—the subconscious mind. People are so generous and sometimes careless or self-serving with their opinions of others and express things to other people with such conviction that an insecure person often believes them. They believe opinions are true and subsequently integrate these opinions into their beliefs about themselves like they are facts. Regardless of any insecurities, the closer people are to us and the more we love and respect them, the easier their opinions slip in and settle as truth. We may remember the words of these people, or we may not, but regardless, the subconscious mind does not miss a beat and records it all. These comments or actions can flow both ways—injecting positive or negative feedback that is a slanted perception that can be interpreted as fact. We may wonder how people can do horrendous things, but their level of awareness, constant exposure to tumultuous environments, and level of soul evolution may cloud their perception of themselves such that they really don't understand the gravity of their actions or they live what they learned. Another possibility is that they have committed to a co-created plan to formidably instigate change and become a disrupter who will ultimately create a world with more compassion and love through actions that deviate from what is accepted or understood by the majority of humans.

In the subconscious recording studio of the mind, falsities stick and can rule the conscious mind and ego until an individual is able to understand what is real and what is not and how the source of their inaccurate or sabotaging beliefs and perceptions were developed. It's not easy to accept new paradigms of being and change belief systems that have guided an individual's steps for many years. Guilt is often the catalyst that motivates a U-turn back to a person's original path or belief system when they begin to question the potential that some of their beliefs have a flawed premise. Sometimes people are exposed to different faiths or philosophies and want to develop their spiritual connection with Oneness differently but feel guilty to proceed. I had clients who requested my assistance when I had my private practice of spiritual counseling and heart-centered hypnotherapy who were afraid to believe anything that deviated from what was instilled as the proper belief system when they grew up, for fear of retribution from their loved ones or from God. They integrated the dogma of the faith they accepted in their youth, but when they were exposed to different philosophies that resonated within them, they experienced guilt that may or may not have prevented them from exploring new beliefs or philosophies. Examples included ideas such as divorce, the possibility of reincarnation, the potential that Jesus had brothers and sisters, or the likelihood that the pope is just a human with great faith but without any more of a direct line to our Creator than we have. There were a few clients I had who grew up Catholic and recognized that they were gay and had difficulty accepting themselves. A few were frightened that they would go to hell if they died. The advice of the Roman Catholic Church to love the sinner and hate the sin scared them and seemed to make it clear that a gay person is a sinner. **The only sin is a lack of love,** and not loving somebody because of their sexual orientation negates Jesus's teachings of love and acceptance. I hope that was a statement from the past and that all people are welcomed in that faith.

The Bible is very much allegorical, and our ability to communicate with spirit did not die over two thousand years ago such that guidance to traverse our present-day challenges cannot be accessed. Politics and religion were indelibly intertwined thousands of years ago, and any documents or words that were not acceptable were banned, and there was the killing and extermination of those groups of people who had other stories that formed the basis of their beliefs. The Roman Catholic Church has a tumultuous history of war, the purpose of which was to ensure that only one message and belief system remained. This message, of course, was not necessarily the correct message. Those with a different messages like the Essenes, Gnostics, Cathars, and so on were considered heretical, and most of them were sought and killed. The Catholic Church was charged with suppressing heresy, and history shows that the first executions for heresy was probably shortly after a decree from Emperor Constantine in around 333 CE and the last was around 1826 CE. That's a lot of years of massacre to shut people up from disagreeing with the dogma of the Catholic Church. I remember reading about the Roman Emperor Constantine many years ago. A brilliant marketing mind, he knew if he embraced and supported the Catholic Church, he could use their incredible infrastructure of priests, bishops, and churches that had a direct line to the people. These networks were scattered across the land from small communities to large, so it was the perfect setup to organize his political messages while simultaneously setting forth and establishing the appropriate doctrines, prayers, rules, and regulations of the Roman Catholic Church. The reason he supported the Catholic Church in the first place was based on death and the winning of battles because he thought Christ was his ally who was assisting him and his armies. He could offer to mandate and maintain the messages of the church through his armies in exchange for his political success. As I mentioned before, he was instrumental in gathering all bishops to come up with the dogma, most of which remains today. The first counsel of Nicaea was convened with the bishops in the city of Nicaea by Constantine. They spent from May until the end of July 325 CE tying up all the loose ends of the Roman Catholic faith that fundamentally remains today.

We now have access to the beliefs of heretics. If you research the Nag Hammadi Library, you will find it is a collection of thirteen ancient books or codices that were discovered in Egypt in 1945. They were found by a farmer and his helpers digging for fertilizer in the Upper Egyptian desert near the town of Nag Hammadi. They were found near the tombs from the Sixth Dynasty of Egypt, under a cliff. This was an incredibly important discovery because those in power thousands of years ago who subscribed to the victorious message with which the Western world is familiar were convinced that any documents to the contrary were destroyed and their beliefs could subsequently be safe in perpetuity without influence from the various groups they considered heretics. The books were hidden to be preserved for the day they were meant to be found—about 1,600 years later. Twelve leather-bound books with pages from a thirteenth volume were found in the earthen jars that were buried and preserved deep into the land. The leather books are made from pages of papyrus bound together, forming forty-six documents in the collection. Among the codices, the Gospels of Thomas, Philip, and Mary are included.

Here is an excerpt from Professor Bart Ehrman's blog, dated August 20, 2018, entitled "What Was Discovered in the Nag Hammadi Library?" He stated that the books include Gospels by such persons as Jesus's disciple Philip and secret revelations delivered to his disciples John and another to James. They include mystical speculations about the beginning of the divine realm and the creation of the world, metaphysical reflections about the meaning of existence, and the glories of salvation. He goes on to state that they include expositions of important religious doctrines and polemical attacks on other Christians for their wrong-headed and heretical views—especially Christians we would call proto-orthodox. He states that the documents are written in Coptic but that there are solid reasons for the thinking that they were each originally composed in Greek.

As always, as with everything that has the potential for controversy, because people are people (always have been, always will be), there have been scholarly debates about the Nag Hammadi documents—but the one single, undeniable truth remains. They were found and they exist and they contain information that eyes had not seen before. They were hidden because the intentions of the powerful were to snuff out any deviation from the message they wanted to rule the future of Christians.

So back to the subconscious mind after my tangent—the clients I had often felt immense pressure to stay the course and resist any deviation from the beliefs that were instilled in them during their youth. Guilt, shame, and unworthiness were among their common emotions or feelings. They are all manifestations of fear, and fear should never be the motivator.

The subconscious mind is the data collector. Think of it as software that runs in the background at all times for every lifetime you have lived. It is the record of the soul. We can't recall our past lives or soul contracts or agreements with ease, but we were created with a built-in system that records our infinite history. The lens through which you view life is primarily created from the product of your earthly lifetime from the fetal stage onward. However, elements of our personalities such as our predilections, talents, temperaments, character traits, and styles of thinking are highly influenced by the aggregate of each soul's experience from each and every lifetime. There are recurrent themes that occur in lifetimes and when developing our soul agreement/co-created plan/soul contracts. We may include various themes we hope to learn to eliminate (like addictions, an abusive nature, extreme submissiveness, etc.) or mitigate (like anger management, intolerance, problematic inflexibility, lack of integrity, bullying, etc.) or enrich (like musical talents, high levels of intuition, etc.). That's why we often reincarnate with individuals who agree to assist us with our soul agreements to learn and evolve mentally, emotionally, and spiritually. The subconscious mind does not reside in conscious memory, but it can influence how we think and act, and this influence can be from any lifetime of the soul. It can be accessed with effort, and usually people seek this therapy when conventional therapy has failed or their minds are open to understand the why of their thoughts or actions that reside outside of their conscious awareness.

The processor or lens of the subconscious mind has no volition and cannot interpret any word, action, or situation. It does not compute if something is in your highest good, good for you, bad for you, irrelevant, and so on. It merely records the history of the soul and all it has experienced within the confines of a physical vehicle or not. I say *or not* because we have had to ability to live in other galaxies or planetary star systems or even reincarnate, if so desired, in nonhuman form. In addition, there is great learning and soul evolution between lifetimes, and those experiences are also recorded. Our free will is quite expansive. The subconscious mind stores history and information that can seem secret to the conscious mind, but it is also possible for fragments of history or events from previous or in-between lives to slip through the cracks of consciousness and undoubtedly affect the lifetime a person is currently living. The conscious mind asks why, and the subconscious mind knows the answer, but answers can only be accessed when it is helpful because the individual must be in a place to accept this knowledge and heal from any former wounds or sources of the issues affecting this lifetime. It's likely the administrator of these potential revelations is under the control of an individual's higher self, as the higher self always knows what is in our best interest for our highest good, and it knows all the reasons.

And this brings us to the exploration of our superconscious mind—also known as our higher self. This element of consciousness maintains the wisdom of the world and understands exactly what is in our best interest in accordance with experiences, soul contracts, and co-created plans. We can access our higher self through love, faith, meditation, and any other activity that veers away from ego and structure and propels us toward spirit. We spent a bit of time discussing the negative ramifications of putting our ego in charge and living a life motivated by structure. When we turn to spirit, we turn to the God within ourselves, our higher self, and that level of consciousness that resides the closest to the Christ Consciousness. The consciousness that was exemplified by the life of the Christ, one of pure love and acceptance.

Understanding consciousness allows us to maintain a better understanding of life. When we understand life, we can navigate challenges because we accept the impermanence of earthly things but acknowledge the permanence of love, divinity, and our soul connections. This is how hope is conceived.

Our higher self is also part of the collective consciousness. Because of the simplicity yet complexity of the collective consciousness, it is difficult to explain using human terminology because humans like to put things into levels, boxes, and categories. Try not to develop a hierarchy in your mind about consciousness. Think of all layers transposed upon each other—like the spiral of time that represents our earthly understanding of time. It's natural to gravitate toward thinking of things in separate compartments and favor the concept of opposites, because it provides a nice, neat simplicity to the understanding of the world. Humans like the idea of compartments and opposites because this type of thinking requires less understanding and enhances the perceived reliance on structure. We have discussed the disadvantages of allowing structure to be the driver of our lives. If we remember that all thoughts and actions take root from love or fear, we acknowledge that hate is a manifestation of fear and a lack of love, not the opposite of any emotion. The spectrum of color is significantly vaster than the human eye can see, but it's easy for a human to judge what seems perfectly sensible to them when it's under their nose in plain view. Many things seem perfectly sensible on earth, but back home, a new world of sounds, color, and vibrancy exists. As with seeing and hearing in the human world, vibration and frequency are keys to understanding the relationship of resonance with the Creator. It's also important to remember that one of the primary properties of light is frequency. I added this to foster thinking outside the box, and I encourage you to explore the level of compartmentalization that you create.

The collective consciousness is the sum total of individual consciousness. It consists of the sum of its parts—the parts being the contributions from each soul in the spirit of Oneness. There are vibrational frequencies related to this consciousness, the richest being, all knowing and all loving, known as the consciousness of God. Deviations from this Source energy are simply changes in harmony or connecting resonance with the Creator. It's difficult to explain because human nature will automatically jump to a concept of levels and separation when you throw out the idea of various vibrations making up the whole. It's easy to lose the concept of Oneness in the process of thinking that way, but go back to how humans just naturally gravitate toward boxes, levels, and opposites—and try to resist. There is only one consciousness of God, one spirit of which we are all comprised as we were made in the image of our Creator, made in, with, and through unconditional love. We are unconditional love, we just have to remember that—a task that seems simple in theory but is not an easy path. We are continually tested on planet earth, and our free will allows us to answer questions and complete our journeys on our own—hence the amnesia, hence a need to truly understand the beauty of what is possible— the recipe of hope that transcends all kinds of frustration and challenges.

Think of the God consciousness as being pure light before it is refracted into parts or frequencies like the colors of the rainbow—colors are easily seen as separate, but a true understanding of light and frequencies allows us to know that every infinitesimal variation of color visible to the naked eye is in fact the refracted frequency from one source. The rainbow may appear separate from the sunlight, but it is not, it is a part of the one big light in the sky.

None of us are separate from each other or from our Creator. It is separation thinking that gets humans into trouble. Every time a human judges themselves or others, they create a condition of separation. They separate themselves and others from the community of love that is an inalienable right gifted by the Creator. Love is unconditional because we were all created from this love, and we are this love—there are no conditions that could take the love away. The idea of being separate continues to establish a barrier between an individual and the Oneness, and it also sets the stage for humans needing intermediaries to help them get to this source of love.

On earth, when we work from the inside out to increase our vibration though remembering and being love, we raise our consciousness. This in turn assists the collective consciousness in raising its aggregate vibration of love and wisdom. As we learn to be more spirit than human and allow our spiritual or higher self to determine and foster our thought processes, we slowly let go of our ego self and our ego becomes more of a servant than a ruler. We are all one—a concept that is difficult for many to comprehend because human words do not adequately explain this concept. It's like when you love somebody so much that words don't exist to qualify or quantify what that love exactly is or how it feels. The important aspect to note is that when we hurt ourselves or someone else, we hurt everyone. In reverse, the more we are love—the more we pour our hearts into the world and the more goodness we exude—the higher we raise the collective consciousness. The higher the aggregate vibration of the collective consciousness, the closer we all get to our Source energy. It's like teamwork of souls in a way—all working for the greater good toward a vibrational goal of pure, unconditional love that envelopes us and aligns us more closely with our Creator. This vibration of love allows greater harmony and resonance among all on earth. It's unconditional because we are made of love, from love, and there is no condition where that can be taken away.

Life on earth is full of conditions. Remember the goal is not to love unconditionally but to be unconditional love—

to live as unconditional love. There is a filament of Source's light within us, and that filament can expand in nature. We have free will and an individual must therefore decide to allow this light to expand on a conscious level. When one wins—we all win!

By virtue of our brotherhood and sisterhood, we also become responsible to globally take part in the rebalancing of the earth's collective consciousness. Everything is affected by this restoration of balance—even weather. We are all connected and are therefore part of the challenge and the resolution. Rebalance is not optional, we truly reap what we sow. Why not sow love, forgiveness, and tolerance and make the world a better place from the inside out.

Chapter Sixteen

Practical Magic

There is no recipe that anyone can give another person to ensure a happy or fulfilled life. There is no formula to sincerely understand a human's purpose and all the elements that make the diamonds of life sparkle—except to genuinely understand the more friction on the diamond, the greater the shine. There is no magic bullet or pill to create or ensure a healthy lifestyle, provide a permanent fix for diet challenges, or clear the clutter that resides within the deepest recesses of our hearts and minds. There is no secret key to unlocking the door to an individual's motivation, self-discipline, or resiliency. There is no mandate to love the self or others because how we think and view the world is completely optional. There is no wand that can be waved to show an individual what life is really like back home and prove that we are all connected by the threads of Oneness and love. There is no time machine that can help closed-minded people understand the motivations and circumstances that surrounded the creation of belief systems from the past. There is, however, love and abundance if you recognize how clandestinely they are often packaged and disguised.

In the words of Burt Bacharach, "What the world needs now is love sweet love, that's the only thing that there's just too little of." Hopefully love will be the springboard to create a happy life, to allow people to understand the nuances of their divine purpose, and to motivate us to be the best we can be. When we understand that what we do to others we do to ourselves and vice versa, we will acknowledge that we are one.

The soul has a limitless capacity to love. Our souls are impervious to death and can access all the wisdom it needs to evolve in perpetuity. We maintain an innate ability to connect to our Creator, the Source of all that is, and we were born with everything we need inside ourselves to feel the connection of love among all earthly and nonearthly things. We have the ability to understand and use the incredible power that resides within, using love to command the universe and allow us to have a constant two-way communication system with the world of spirit and the creation of hope. Love commands the universe, and we are love. The God we seek cannot be found externally, it can only be found internally, within the recesses of our heart, mind, and spirit.

According to the Oxford Languages, "Magic is defined as the power of apparently influencing the course of events by using mysterious or supernatural forces." What makes anything look like it happened magically is the lack of awareness or understanding of how any event or circumstance was orchestrated. Miracles happen every day, and some cannot be explained with human thoughts or words, but an open mind can often do the trick.

A few days after my dad died, I decided to wear a pair of pants to work that were in my oldest daughter's former room. They were in her large black dresser with five drawers, and the condition of the dresser was perfect. As I've said before, I can hear my dad speak to me, and I can usually feel his presence or influence. When I came home from work that day and went into that bedroom to put my pants back in the drawer, I noticed this oily substance on all the drawers except the last drawer and legs of the dresser. My first thought was *oh no—what did I have in the top drawer that leaked all over?* I started to remove every item from each drawer, and I began to wipe this unknown, oily-but-not-really-oily substance. My youngest daughter was home at the time and heard the commotion of emptying all the drawers and swearing about what the heck leaked. She came into the bedroom to help me take everything out of the drawers and wipe this unknown substance. When we got to the last drawer, we found there was absolutely nothing but clothes in every drawer, and there was no liquid of any kind in any of the drawers. She looked at me quizzically and I responded, "Poppey walked through this dresser to let us know he's here and around and can do new tricks!" To this day, she tells me that unless she was there to witness this, she'd find it very hard to believe me. I smelled and even tasted the substance—it was unfamiliar in every way. It wasn't really oily, although it appeared that way, and it didn't taste or smell of anything. After we cleaned all the drawers, inside and out, we were amazed that there was no staining, streaks, or remnants of any kind. Any piece of clothing that had this substance on it was unstained and not changed. The drops of this substance floated on top of any clothing and didn't penetrate the material like oil or water would have. Even the next day and thereafter, the black dresser had no marks or smudges or anything unusual because of this supernatural event. This substance is called ectoplasm. Ectoplasm is a manifestation of spiritual energy. When we have "interesting" events happen to us, such as flickering lights, the presence of special numbers, visits by birds, butterflies and animals or music popping out of nowhere via songs carrying a special meaning that find their way onto our playlists, and so on, we should never doubt the supernatural or magical nature of these gifts. At sixty-five years old, when I was out training for my last marathon, I was running my first seventeen-mile run, and I was having trouble completing the last few miles—I reached out to Dale (he trained with me) to give me a boost of energy. Shortly after, I noticed ectoplasm on my hand. I had to stop to think if I wiped my nose or something, but I hadn't—LOL—it was just a kind reminder that he was there, putting in the miles with me. If a person pays attention, there are signs everywhere that those who have died whom we love are near, and they want to express their love and presence. The dresser was by far the wildest event that occurred to date. When I met with a medium shortly after I asked, "Dad, the dresser?" He responded, "Yes, that was me, but I think I went a bit too far on that one!" Also of note, all those in the world of spirit who visit us are at least a couple of feet off the ground—that's why the last drawer and legs of the dresser were unaffected. Magic? Only to those who can't believe. Many stories exist about apparitions of the Blessed Mother and statues of her crying oil . . . a gift to all who know. Divine, supernatural events happen frequently. We all must always keep an eye and ear out!

There are other helpful tools in life that seem to work by magic. For example, my pendulum and I have a very trusted and sound relationship. I use body dowsing to ensure that the minerals and vitamins I take are in my best interest, and when I want to know if I should avoid some food, I body dowse for the answers. Those who don't understand dowsing may think it foolish to trust in such a source of information, but in actuality, it is a gift that was bestowed by our earth and Creator, and it is founded in science. Dowsing for water lines and water has been done for centuries. It's all about awareness and understanding. I order a lot online—I really don't like to go shopping often. If I'm unsure of the size, I use kinesiology to assist. I can't even think of a time I used it and received the wrong size. There are so many tools at our disposal that elude most people walking the earth. I've explained that we are beings of energy and that we have electric currents and subsequent bioelectric fields produced around us. Why would such a gift be of limited value? Wouldn't you think there was a greater purpose than just having them exist?

Let me explain some of this practical magic that may be useful to navigate life. Dowsing is an example of another powerful illustration of a human body's sensitivity to subtle energies. The more we understand vibrational energies, the more the realization of innate tools will surface. For centuries dowsers have located underground water and minerals. The indication of water is just that—an indication. The real deal is the layout of the human body, the technology of our nervous and circulatory systems to create electric currents and our ability to tune into the electromagnetic fields of the earth, our higher selves, and the collective consciousness. Just as I explained with Reiki, these are innate tools that can be accessed by knowing about their existence. Dowsing is an act of resonance. We can gather a great deal of wisdom from dowsing. It's a paradigm shift for many to believe in the bioelectric fields of humans and nature such that our environment can provide significant fields of information. Our consciousness and collective consciousness play an important participatory role in this plethora of knowledge and wisdom.

If one invests in a pendulum, it's best to carry it around for a few days so that it integrates your energy or frequencies into the pendulum. When I taught Reiki and I'd illustrate the rotation and placement of our major chakras in the body, I always had a separate pendulum to use for class so everyone could share it. My pendulum sits on my meditation altar, and I don't let anyone use it—some people carry their pendulums at all times. Prior to using a pendulum it's good to ask if it's a good time to discuss whatever issue you plan on addressing. For years prior and periodically today, I ask it to confirm yes and no movements by saying, "Show me yes. Stop. Show me no." For me, questions about anything that is a fact, happened in the past, or reflects the current conditions are spot on—and I use my pendulum whenever I need to access wisdom outside my knowing. For example, during my marathon training, I had my pendulum tell me how many miles were in my best interest to run that day instead of sticking to a usual running plan. I used it to tell me when to wrap my Achilles tendon in KT tape. I asked about clothing, and so on. At sixty-five, there are nuances not addressed in general running programs, but my pendulum knows what's best for me. I don't ask future questions unless I preface it with, "At this time, is _____ in alignment with the possibilities that exist today?" The future is malleable due to everyone's free will, so requesting answers about the future is often a gamble. I've sometimes learned the hard way that my questions were not specific enough, and I received the correct answer to something I wasn't actually asking. With time, practice, and trust, I have come to find it an extremely valuable resource.

When body dowsing, I stand straight, with soft knees, the crown of my head extended as high as I can reach (the part of your head where a ponytail would be), relaxed shoulders, and abdominal muscles engaged with the rest of my body totally relaxed. I will place the food or supplement at my solar plexus (center of my chest, just below the sternum or breastbone, above the diaphragm). Then I read my body by the sway—forward sway means yes, backward tip means no, and no sway forward or back means no harm, no good, so you can go with your preference. I can't tell you the number of people I've taught this too—they are amazed. Do the exercise with a sugar packet and an apple and see how they compare!

When using kinesiology, I apply pressure to my index finger while it's extended and my fist rests flatly on a solid surface. I actually learned this when I received PSYCH-K training. I always start by stating that my name is something other than my name, and then restating that my name is Maryann Roefaro. If the system is working and able, you will not be able to bend your finger when a truthful statement is made. If your finger bends both with truth and fiction, drink some water. A person needs to be fully hydrated to use this methodology because the flow of energy is paramount. It's amazing how much pressure you can place on your index finger and it will not move when a truthful statement is made.

Continuing with the practical magic of our bodies, as a reminder, a chakra is an energy center within the body that has an impact on our physical, mental, emotional, and spiritual well-being. Chakra is a Sanskrit word that means "wheel" or "disk." A balanced chakra is open and rotates freely within its energetic patterns. If you picture your face to be a clock, the chakras rotate clockwise. During times of stress or injury a chakra may be closed (not rotating freely), inhibited, or out of balance. A practitioner can feel these conditions by training their hands to understand the nuances of energetic patterns. Chakras that are closed will be cool or cold, but when they are opened and rotating correctly, a lovely flow of energy can be felt. If you think you are incapable of feeling energy, just rub your palms together and pay attention to what you feel in the palms of your hands as you gradually separate them, farther and farther away from each other. When you can no longer feel the energy, they will go cold. With practice you can feel energy bounce from one palm to the other, and you can stretch it and play with the energy to teach your hands how to feel the patterns! An individual can rebalance their chakras through intention. A Reiki or vibrational medicine provider acts as a conduit to assist people to heal themselves through entrainment and all the other scientific principles we discussed earlier. Each chakra vibrates to a different frequency, hence, the frequencies of various colors. Knowing the placement and colors of the chakras, an individual can meditate to open and balance each chakra to be consistent with their highest good. I have provided an explanation of the color and location of each major chakra in the body. Following that I have provided a meditation that may be helpful to rebalance your energy centers yourself. You can always read through the meditation and elect to voice record it, so you can close your eyes and be fully present to assist yourself in this innate gift of love.

At the base of the spine, sitting in the delicate bowl of the pelvis, is a chakra that vibrates to the frequency of the color red. This is called the root chakra. It's located in the seat of the body because it's rooted deeply in humanness. This chakra can be out of whack from normal daily living and traversing the challenges of everyday life, or it can be closed or out of balance because it maintains energetic memory of significant childhood wounds, insecurities, family issues, or security or safety concerns to name a few.

Next up is the sacral chakra. It's located between the belly button and the root chakra. This chakra vibrates to the frequency of the color orange. Like the root chakra, this can be out of balance from daily living and traversing the challenges of everyday life. Among other connections, this sacral chakra is energetically connected to the cells, tissues, and organs that surround the area. It is also associated with relationships, including relationships with abundance and money. There could be circulating feelings of tension, animosity, or other dysfunctions with people that you love, an unhealthy relationship with your job or career, or even feelings of a lack of abundance associated with not having enough money to pay bills that need to be healed.

Next up is the solar plexus chakra. It's located in the vicinity of the solar plexus, close to the end of the sternum near the xiphoid process. The solar plexus chakra vibrates to the frequency of the color yellow. Among other connections, the solar plexus is an energy center that is a point of entry that gathers external energy from the universal life force. I find that easy to remember because yellow reminds me of the color of the sun. The sun is a precious ball of energy that can be seen and felt from all over the planet. No matter where anyone is on earth, they are united by their ability to connect to the one sun that bathes all of us in warmth and light. The balance of this chakra is often associated with feelings of the self—an individual's view of themselves, their self-worth, or self-esteem.

Next up is the heart chakra. It's located near the heart but is more central to the invisible vertical axis that splits the body into two equal parts. The heart chakra connects humanness to spirit. Some call it the spiritual root chakra since so much exchange of divinity occurs around that location. The actual heart muscle is the first to form in any fetus, and life ceases when this muscle rests and no longer pumps the life-sustaining oxygen and nutrients to keep the body alive. It's no wonder it's often referred to as the seat of the soul. The energy that emanates from the electrical current provided by the pumping heart is one of the major players in the formation of the energetic web that surrounds the body—often referred to as the aura or energetic field. The heart chakra is associated with the frequency that corresponds to the vibration of the color green. When somebody feels their heart is broken, the energy of the heart chakra is significantly affected. Emotional issues are the number one cause of heart chakras being out of balance. Sometimes, as balance begins to be attained at the heart chakra, an individual will have an emotional release and start crying—they may not even know why they are crying. The heart chakra can hold millennia of emotions through cell memory. It's the chakra most closely associated with compassion and tolerance. When we create the conditions for a joy-filled life, the energy of this chakra is essential in those feelings of joy and our capacity for us to love ourselves and others.

Next up is the throat chakra, and that's where it's located, in the area of the throat/neck, in the vicinity of a man's Adam's apple. This is a human's center of truth and self-expression. It is not uncommon for the throat chakra to be out of balance when a person has not been honest with themselves—when they have wanted to but have not spoken the words they feel they should to some person, or they are holding back regarding some situation. These expressions may not always be verbal as those who cannot speak can still harbor feelings that create a lack of individual authenticity. The throat chakra vibrates to the frequency associated with the color blue and is indelibly intertwined with our ability to communicate—both verbally and nonverbally.

Next up is the mind's eye or third eye chakra, associated with the vibration of the color indigo or violet. This is one of the chakras most in communication with all that is divine. It is located between the eyebrows, behind the forehead. When exercised through meditation, yoga, or other spiritual traditions, it will be like a muscle that becomes more powerful, strong and ready to be activated at any time. The minds-eye is where many can see things and beings of a spiritual nature. During meditation it is not uncommon to feel or see this chakra as a crystalline structure of divine facets. It's a center of love, devotion, divine communication, intuition, and knowing. It possesses the highest frequency intervals. It is a chakra that can assist in directing a human to understand their purpose, directions, decisions, and thoughts in life. It can provide energetic alignment to allow an individual to know they are in the right place at the right time—or in the right place, doing the right thing . . . and vice versa.

The seventh major chakra is the crown. This chakra is located a few inches above the crown of the head of both humans and animals. It is associated with the colors deep violet or white or even white with gold. It is the chakra of Oneness. It can provide a sense of connection to our Creator and all that is—connecting with the universe in a sacred bond providing spiritual awareness.

Did you notice the color sequence? Red, orange, yellow, green blue, indigo/violet—does that ring a bell? The major chakras match the colors of the rainbow, and as their vibration differs from person to person, the shade or hue of the color changes to make up the rainbow of earth's existence. If this is a surprise to you, you will probably never look at a rainbow the same. When you see your next rainbow, you will likely study the variations in color so you'll become more familiar with the shades of the chakras! Here's another interesting fact—the frequencies are also associated with sound or musical notes. Can you guess what order that would be? The scale of C is the root chakra, and it goes to D, E, F, G, A, B! There are additional chakras—even outside the human body and within the energetic web that surrounds the body. You can probably guess that the sounds just continue in harmonic resonance! If you think all this is a coincidence—think again!

If an individual wishes to rebalance or open their chakras without a practitioner, meditation is the key to success. Here is one example of a meditation to use:

Find a quiet place with no noise or someplace with relaxing music you are fond of and sit in a yoga position, on a chair, or wherever and however you are comfortable. Lengthen your spine to a position of good posture. You can do this by lifting the crown of your head while seated (not the top of your head—the crown, which is farther back where a high ponytail would sit) and feel the decompression of your spine and the engagement of your lower abdominal muscles. Make sure your neck and shoulders are relaxed. Relax your entire body. It's likely your core muscles will be engaged to keep your spine decompressed but make every effort to relax everything. Begin breathing consciously with deep inhalations and exhalations. When you feel your body is relaxed, begin your personal energy-rebalancing session. If your face were a clock, the chakras would spin in the direction of the hands of the clock, from noon at your forehead to six at your chin. That is direction of the visual spinning that you will you imagine.

Set your intention. You may say it to yourself or out loud. As I suggested previously, you can even record this on your phone and play it back during your meditation session. Don't fret if you don't meditate—I will keep your heart and mind engaged and active, and you're in charge of keeping your body relaxed and your breathing deep and cleansing. Create your intention, perhaps something like these. I am created from love, and therefore I am love. Love commands the universe. Love gives me the ability to heal myself by allowing the universal life force of love and light to enter my body. I command every cell in my body to awaken to the vibration of love and light of our Creator. I command every cell in my body to vibrate to the perfection of Oneness. I command every cell to vibrate at the frequency of perfection, to the frequency of Oneness, where only health and wellness is sustainable.

Allow your crown chakra to connect with the universal life force through your intention—just say it is so! Visualize and allow a white light with tiny, iridescent gold, pink, blue, and green specks to enter the crown of your head and flow through your body into the floor, through the ground, all the way to the center of the earth (where it's recycled and purified to return to the life force). Visualize this channel or column of light expanding. Allow the circumference of the column to expand and envelop the body. Allow the light to form a field or column of light that extends about three feet from the extremities of the body (as if you had your arms outstretched to the edge of the column of light). Visualize this light flowing at whatever speed your mind takes it—through the channel—into the center of the earth. As it flows, allow the light, using your intention, to cleanse your body from all that is causing discomfort—thoughts, feelings, emotions, and physical issues. When you feel that the column of light has completed whatever it was to do (your intuition will tell you), continue with the remainder of the meditation.

Bring your attention to the root chakra. Visualize a beautiful red bolus of spinning light, rotating in the direction I explained previously in the location of the root chakra, at the base of the spine, filling the pelvic area. Visualize this precious red light spinning as a wheel of energy, and imagine this energy produced from this spinning light of love cleansing all the cells, tissues, and organs in its vicinity. Know you are made from love and love commands the universe. There is no question, your body will absolutely respond to your commands. Allow the flow of this red healing light to heal any feelings related to a lack of safety or security. If you have wounds from your early years, bring them to mind and allow the light to consume any negative feelings, and allow yourself to forgive the past and begin healing those wounds. If you have any family or work issues that make you feel unsafe or insecure in your activities of daily living, allow the swirling red light to consume and transform these feelings into a place of love and security. Allow the spinning to become brighter and fill the space with love. Allow the light to heal and cleanse to the level that is currently possible within your highest good and capacity to know and heal. Sometimes issues are like peeling onion skins—one layer a time. A release may be felt—or just a wave of greater peace and new hope of resolution. When your intuition tells you to move to the next chakra, just listen and follow the guidance of your higher, divine self.

Bring your attention to the sacral chakra. Visualize a beautiful orange bolus of spinning light at the location of the sacral chakra. As a reminder, it's about halfway between your belly button and root chakra. Visualize this loving orange light spinning and imagine the energy from this spinning light is cleansing all the cells, tissues, and organs in its vicinity. Know you are made from love and love commands the universe. There is no question, your body will absolutely respond to your commands. Allow the flow of this orange healing light to heal any feelings related to relationships of all kinds that bother you. Recall any relationships you feel are burdens that you carry every

day. It could be a relationship with money—feeling difficulty paying rent or feeding your family—or it could be
some difficulty you are experiencing with a spouse, child,
family member, friend, or foe. Feel the love healing all that
is troubling you. Also ask for healing from any issues that
may exist at a level of consciousness of which you remain
unaware but fuel the self-talk that feeds your existence. Allow the light to consume and transmute negative feelings
and allow yourself to forgive or gain greater confidence
in the abundant universe to allow the light to begin healing your discomforts. Allow the swirling orange light to
consume and transform any negative feelings into a place
of love and peace. Allow the spinning light to become
brighter and fill the space with love. When your intuition
tells you to move to the next chakra, just listen and follow
the guidance of your higher, divine self.

Bring your attention to the solar plexus chakra. Visualize a powerful bolus of yellow spinning light at the location of the solar plexus chakra. As a reminder, it's located
below the sternum near the xiphoid process. Visualize a
vibrant, strong, resilient, and loving yellow light spinning
and imagine the energy from this spinning light is cleansing all the cells, tissues, and organs in its vicinity. Know
you are made from love and love commands the universe.
There is no question, your body will absolutely respond to
your commands. Allow the flow of this yellow healing light
to fortify your feelings of self-confidence and self-assured-
ness and allow it to heal any feelings related to negative
thoughts about the self. Allow the spinning yellow light to
feed every cell in your body with the power that resides
within the self. Feel the power—feel powerful to overcome
any challenge and know you have the tools to overcome
and succeed. Know you have the power to stand in your
authenticity and be resilient through all challenges. Feel

the power of love heal any negative feelings about the self. Ask for healing from any issues that may exist at a level of consciousness outside your awareness but fuel the self-talk that feeds your existence in a manner that is not conducive to your highest good. Allow the light to consume and transmute negative feelings and allow yourself to forgive and accept your human frailties and see the perfection and beauty. Allow self-love to become magnified and feel the power fueling your healing. Allow the swirling yellow light to consume and transform any negative feelings and catapult them into a place of love and peace. Allow the spinning light to become brighter and fill the space with love. When your intuition tells you to move to the next chakra, just listen and follow the guidance of your higher, divine self.

Bring your attention to the heart chakra. Visualize the most loving and compassionate bolus of green spinning light at the location of the heart chakra. As a reminder, it's located close to the heart but more central to the chest area. Visualize a deeply loving green light spinning and imagine the energy from this spinning light is cleansing all the cells, tissues, and organs in its vicinity. Know you are made from love and love commands the universe. There is no question, your body will absolutely respond to your commands. Allow the flow of this green loving light to feel like a cup runneth over such that the love instantaneously bathes each cell in the body with divine love. Allow the loving green light to feed every cell in your body with the infinite supply of love that is found within. Know that this infinite supply is always present and ready when you need it. Feel the intense love—feel the love to allow you to create the conditions for joy and a life filled with tolerance and inner peace. Feel the power of love heal any feelings of loss or sadness. Allow love to heal negative feelings about the self or anyone. Allow any heartbreak to be healed. If your heart requires healing from loss due to the death of a loved one, feel that loved one nearby. See them smile and feel their love. Perhaps you can visualize them laughing. Know that at this frequency of relaxation and meditation that you have achieved from this exercise, a connection with the light bodies of those back home is facilitated. Ask for healing from any issues that may exist at a level of consciousness outside your awareness but fuel the self-talk that feeds your existence in a manner that is not conducive to your highest good. Allow the light to consume and transmute negative feelings and allow yourself to forgive and accept your human frailties and see the perfection and beauty within the self. Allow self-love to become magnified and feel the power of this love fuel healing. Allow the swirling green light to consume and transform any negative feelings and catapult them into a place of love and compassion. Allow the spinning light to become brighter and fill the space with love. When your intuition tells you to move to the next chakra, just listen and follow the guidance of your higher, divine self.

Bring your attention to the throat chakra. Visualize an authentic and loving bolus of blue spinning light at the location of the throat chakra. As a reminder, it's located in the area of the throat/swallowing area. Visualize a vibrant blue light spinning and imagine the energy from this spinning light cleansing all the cells, tissues, and organs in its vicinity. Know you are made from love and love commands the universe. There is no question, your body will respond to your commands. Allow the flow of this blue healing light to yield a sense of power and strength that ignites the courage and power within to recognize and be proud of your authentic self. Allow the light to provide illumination to step into your truth and self-realization. See yourself as the love in which you exist. Know that you have the tools and ability to speak your truth, stand up for your beliefs, protect the precious gift to the world that your existence brings, and be proud to be you. Allow the spinning blue light to feed every cell in your body with the power that resides within the self. Allow the light to consume and transmute negative feelings and allow yourself to forgive and accept your human frailties and see the perfection and beauty. Allow self-love to become magnified and feel the power to stand in your truth. Allow the swirling blue light to consume and transform any negative feelings and catapult them into a place of love and peace. Allow the spinning light to become brighter and fill the space with love. When your intuition tells you to move to the next chakra, just listen and follow the guidance of your higher, divine self.

Bring your attention to the third eye chakra. Visualize divine light of indigo/violet spinning at the location of the third eye chakra. As a reminder, it's located between the eyebrows behind the forehead. Visualize a vibrant indigo/violet light spinning and imagine the energy from this spinning light is cleansing all the cells, tissues, and organs in its vicinity. Know you are made from love and love commands the universe. There is no question, your body will respond to your commands. Allow the flow of this indigo/violet healing light to yield a sense of connection to spirit. Feel the love of the universe and all that is divine. Allow the love and divine connection to vibrate through your entire body. Acknowledge and accept that your intuition is a gift that can be used at any time to illuminate and guide your path. Trust that your higher, divine self possesses all the wisdom you need to answer your questions and solve any dilemmas. Remember what this feels like and be confident that with practice you can access the gifts of the mind's eye chakra and your intuition at a moment's notice. Allow the indigo/violet light to consume and transmute any self-doubt and foster a trust in your intuition and continuous connection to spirit. With each breath, allow the light to become deeper in hue and fill all the cells of your body with love. When your intuition tells you to move to the next chakra, just listen and follow the guidance of your higher, divine self.

Bring your attention to the crown chakra. Visualize divine light of spinning iridescent white light with specks of gold or silver or pink or blue at the location of the crown chakra. Allow your intuition to select the colors and therefore vibrations that are best for your highest good at this moment in time. As a reminder, the crown chakra is located about three to six inches above the crown of the head. Visualize this iridescent white light with shimmering specks spinning and flowing over and through your entire body. Know you are made from love and love commands the universe. There is no question, your body will respond to your commands. Allow the flow of this white light to yield a sense of connection to the universe, Creator, and the world of Oneness. Feel the love of the Source of all that is—our Creator, our God—and know that this love of which you were created and will be, throughout infinity, forever without end. Allow the love and divine connection to vibrate through your entire body. Allow this unconditional love to consume and transmute anything that falls outside of your highest good. With each breath, allow the light to glisten and continue to flow and illuminate your being. Feel the Oneness of all that is—bathe in this light and love until your intuition tells you it's time to open your eyes. Don't be surprised if when you open your eyes, your surroundings are extremely bright. Allow this feeling of love and peace to linger and make a decision to have a great day!

With practice, this self-care and rebalancing of the chakras can take as much time as you have or want to put forth. If you only have three minutes, you'll know how to accomplish this in three minutes. If you balance your energies on a regular basis, it will keep your first line of defense intact and improve your immunity to just about everything . . . including the toxic humans you may encounter. When you get really familiar with the colors and your own personal rebalancing technique, you can do it without meditating . . . while you're running for example!

Chapter Seventeen
Faith, Hope, and Charity

Self-mastery is the one key to unlocking the potential for enlightenment within us, as through the mastery of our minds, body, and spirit we deepen our indelible connection to spirit and our Creator Mother-Father God, and we enrich our love vibration to become closer to the consciousness of God.

Faith is a belief in our Source that allows us to go beyond human reason and accept that which is divine and defies gravity. Hope is knowing that things are not always what they appear to be, and regardless of what seems to be happening before us, all is in perfect order in accordance with our co-created plan and co-created plans of others, in divine concert with our Source, and there's a reason for everything. Charity is the knowing that unconditional love is an act of being and not an act of doing, and we can make a choice to live as love and continually ask ourselves what love would say and do.

Although there isn't a map that I can provide for you to find your pot of gold, perhaps I can summarize some of the concepts we discussed in this book by reflecting upon the potential for their practical application. Believe in yourself, be brave, and know you have choices. You must be your biggest fan and advocate. Be the observer and act as your wise and trusted friend and adviser. Dig deeply to identify the changes you need to simplify your life to reduce stress and anxiety. Be honest and be prepared to make the decisions that are in your highest good, not the highest good of others or within the belief systems of other people. Be prepared to forgive. It's essential to let go of any ill feelings or negative emotions such as anger, frustration, dislike, or disappointment with another person. It's imperative to heal the part of the self that allows others to stir up negative feelings and upset. Communication is a two-way street and sometimes signals can get crossed. Whatever the reasons, harboring ill feelings like anger or resentment can have a negative impact on the person holding on to those feelings and emotions, not on the person to whom they are directed. The individual to whom the anger, resentment, and so on is placed remains unaffected, but the negativity poisons the self through that toxic relationship with those feelings. The words or events that caused the issue to spark in the first place cannot be reversed and the clock can't be turned back. The only option is forgiveness of the self and others and movement onward to create a new day that will ultimately result in the healing of negative feelings.

So how will you know when you are on the right track and your self-mastery journey is leading you to a level of consciousness that indicates you are reaping the rewards of your efforts and love rules more than ego?

- You love and like yourself more every day. With each passing day, when you look in the mirror—despite any new imperfections or wrinkles—you love the reflection you see because you see much more than a face; you see a heart center that beats with love and has a palpable passion for life and mankind. You have developed a sense of the light you can provide to the world, and with all your flaws, you cut yourself slack and say, good job—keep it up! You are kind to yourself, and most importantly, you trust yourself. You consistently tap into your intuition and use it to guide your steps. You know when you are in balance or aligned and when you are not—and when you are not, you have developed the tools to redirect yourself in a positive and loving manner. You have control of your thoughts, and you find yourself consistently spending a few minutes in solitude, sometimes even in a crowd or on a busy highway.

- You appreciate your hands and feet and all that is in between. You really appreciate who you have become. You have pride in all that you do because it's commonplace to autograph your work with excellence. You don't compromise your integrity and are not driven by material wealth. You notice your needs seem to be taken care of because the universe responds to your directions because they are seeded in love. Because of your expansion of self-love, you find it easier to protect yourself against self-sabotage. You have developed a level of understanding about healthy living, and you know what your body needs and how best to take care of it because of the level of love and appreciation you have for this precious vessel that envelops your everlasting spirit.

- You appear to bring light to situations. Somehow, when dealing with your own issues or helping others, you are inspired with advice and answers that you know are of divine origin and they flow and come to you easily. You don't harbor hidden agendas and your dedication to building a better humanity is transparent. People gravitate toward you because at some level of consciousness, they feel your love. You bring light where there is darkness. You bring comfort where there is pain. You bring joy where there is sadness. You bring reality where there is fantasy. You bring love where there is discourse. You are strong and impervious to negative comments and negative energy. Your wisdom doesn't allow you to fall off the ledge through negativity and doesn't swell your ego through positivity. You are steadfast in your belief in yourself and Oneness, yet you continually realize you don't have the complete dataset and don't know everything—that some of your premises may be flawed and therefore your mind is always open.

- You speak your truth, and honesty becomes the word and habit of the day. You understand and know that there is no reason to not speak your truth and that truth provides freedom. You can say no without guilt. You can put yourself first and it's OK because you've realized that when your vessel is full, it can be of much help to others. You understand that sometimes the truth is difficult to communicate to those we may love and those we don't even like, but you are strong enough to say what you feel is necessary. You say it with love using your heart center and not your ego. You are not perfect by any means, but you accept yourself and others. There are people who make you uncomfortable and vibrate to a frequency that you're not interested in hanging out with, so you've made decisions to limit your exposure to anyone who drains your energy and makes you feel bad. You've begun to understand that there are reasons far beyond your knowing as to how and why individuals become products of their environment, and you try your best not to judge. You try not to judge but rather choose to follow your intuition and limit your exposure to those whose densities make you feel uncomfortable. You're OK with those limits, regardless of who the people are. You understand that you will not love everyone, but you can detach to have respect for all humanity and wish them prosperity and love in their self-mastery journey.

- You seem to consistently see the beauty and goodness in people, situations, and your surroundings. Others tell you things about people that you have not noticed because your eyes, ears, and heart seek the good, and that's what you can see. When you're out in nature, the love you feel for the earth and the universe is beyond words. The sights, smells, and sounds of nature feed your soul and allow you to feel the Oneness of our precious existence.

- Your commitment to stewardship grows more deeply with each passing day, and you have developed a "service" orientation. In your personal or professional journey, you may feel more compelled to do good things for your community. You find that giving to others is natural and it provides a greater sense of wholeness. Giving can include volunteering, serving on community boards and committees, or providing financial assistance. It's almost impossible to traverse the self-mastery journey and not feel such gratitude for all of life's gifts that lead to giving and sharing through love. There is a saying attributed to Buddha, "Your work is to discover your world and then with all your heart give yourself to it." Love means even more when it's shared.

- Maybe you have noticed that you seem to crave more time alone. As you develop in your self-mastery journey, time for contemplation or meditation becomes more desirable. It may even become a necessary component of each day. The time with the self can happen anywhere. Alone time is important to clear the clutter and help the mind and body remain impervious to negative influences and energies. It's often easier to prepare the body to be impervious to the impending day instead of scraping the crap off at the end. No person escapes life unscathed from the daily stresses, responsibilities, obligations, and tasks that need to be accomplished on a daily basis. Use the meditative techniques provided in previous chapters to assist in this process—you can lengthen and shorten them to meet your needs.

- With time, when you actually stop to think about it, you notice you spend less and less precious time contemplating or debating about who was right or who was wrong because forgiveness flows much more easily—not only forgiveness of the self, but also the forgiveness of others. It's really important to understand that all people, given the tools and level of conscious awareness and soul evolution of that they vibrate, are just doing the best they can at any time. When you understand that everything you think, feel, say, and do comes from how you view yourself and from what's inside, you know without a doubt that it's not valid, necessary, or appropriate to take anything personally. People who hurt others through greed, selfishness, ignorance, or other forms of unawareness may not know how to be different. This is why the universe maintains the role to rebalance. Just take care of yourself and allow the universe to do its job; the universe re-balances as appropriate, no exceptions. There is no personal retaliation necessary. The legal ram-ifications of one's actions are usually addressed by the infrastructure established in communities through law and order. There is no reason to har-bor grudges or hurt ourselves by carrying nega-tivity around. Negativity doesn't change anything; it just pollutes our inner peace and harmony.

- It may seem that people apologize for saying or doing something that may have previously regis-tered with you but doesn't anymore. The self-mas-tery journey allows you to maintain a new loving awareness of the self and not assume things you may have previously. With mastery, you don't take things personally. A by-product of loving is accepting and trusting people's intentions. If you have trust that a person's intentions are good, things they say or do don't have the same effect they used to. You recognize that the person may be having a bad day or just not liking themselves at the moment, so things don't always come out of people's mouths that are loving. The further along the self-mastery journey, the more impervious a human becomes to the day-to-day turmoil, turbulence, and drama that people create. Some people are just plain drama creators—and those who are evolved will recognize this and either allow the drama to go in one ear and out the other or they will just limit their exposure to negativity. As the self-mastery journey is enriched, we maintain a greater ability to contemplate, understand, and trust people's intentions. We can understand more clearly that although all are in different places on their journey, they're doing the best that they can given their current state of self-evolution.

- As the mastery journey progresses, the Oneness of all can be felt more intensely. The knowing and feeling of divinity is all around us, and when we are aware, it's a palpable presence. This knowing of Oneness promotes a greater spirituality, as we know spirituality develops from the inside out. Those in a state of developing mastery often focus less on dogma and more on spirit—trusting their intuition, instincts, and knowing. It's a beautiful feeling knowing we are never alone, and we really do have an army of dedicated helpers that will illuminate our path and carry us when we stumble and fall.

- As the mastery journey continues, an individual may crave simplicity. They may want their environments to be free of clutter and congestion. It's often easier to think when we have space—including space in our day.

- When mastery approaches, negativity feels bad and any old patterns of negativity dissolve. The new way of living is driven more by spirit and the higher self and less by ego. An individual becomes more sensitive to negative energy and makes every effort to minimize or eliminate it from life. This can often mandate difficult decisions with re- lationships, family, living conditions, and so on.

- When a person has been on this jour- ney, it is evident to everyone that there is much less drama and negativity in their life.

- Because love commands the universe, the jour- ney of self-mastery fosters the cooperation with the forces or principles of life. This allows life to take on a greater "ease." Thoughts are manifest- ed more easily, divine coincidences occur natural- ly and more frequently, and love-based thoughts rule instead of negatively charged thoughts. Life is filled with more peace and joy. The con- ditions for a joy-filled life, even in the face of challenge, are created and the result is seen and felt by all. There is greater ease to life when love rules. The self-mastery journey is fundamentally a trajectory toward understanding how to allow love to command our lives—from the inside out.

- As an individual gains self-mastery, the act of putting the self first becomes more natural and does not create guilt or feelings of inadequacy. Humans find it difficult to believe when they're traveling on an airplane with small children that they're supposed to put their oxygen mask on first and then help them—at first blush, it seems self-ish and inappropriate. However, when you realize that you can't help anyone if you're not breath-ing, it makes sense. A well cannot quench thirst if it's empty. It takes time to get the gist of taking care of the self so that the self can be ready to serve others. When a person is happy, balanced, well-nourished, and rested, they can do great things. If a person is beat up, exhausted, over-worked, burned out, and hungry they will sure-ly lack the creativity and fortitude to help them-selves and others. It's essential to put the self first because when everything is good on the inside, it's good on the outside. When all people main-tain peace within, there will be peace on earth.

- As the self-mastery journey continues, the pull to solve everybody's problems diminishes and fades into the past. Understanding the co-created plan means understanding that the only way a person can learn the lessons and gifts they put in their path is to figure it out themselves. We are not here to solve other people's problems and fix all the issues they create. We are here to love and support each other's plans—for the greater good of the whole and the attainment of the highest level of consciousness. When we have an oppor-tunity to help others by facilitating the resolution of challenges through the removal of boulders or icebergs, we help them to help themselves. By using our wisdom and resources to empow-er them, we helped them get the clutter out of their way. This assists others to develop the life skills to build resilience and fortitude. Solving other people's challenges for them only means the lesson remains to be learned at another time.

- If a person allows their spirit self or higher self to be in control of their human mind, body, and spirit on a regular basis, an individual's needs seem to be met—miraculously. Allowing spirit to dominate over the human ego provides a continual channel between a person and all that is divine. The army of angels, divine beings, ascended masters, saints, and prophets—all beings of light— are accessible at the speed of thought. When the spirit or divine self is in charge, everything from thoughts to actions can be influenced in a manner that is consistent with the highest good of the individual's physical, mental, emotional, and spiritual well-being. The person's vibration of love continues to develop such that the manifestation of goodness often seems miraculous. The only effort or work that is needed is a sincere, genuine, and unequivocal knowing of Oneness and the role humanity plays in this myriad of love. The rest will just happen as the roads in life will curve and turn in the direction that serves an individual and the whole closest to the will of our Source. Love commands the universe, and grace is one of the tangible gifts bestowed by our Creator.

- As an individual traverses their self-mastery journey, even the most analytical minds become more tolerant and accepting of that which is not black and white. The gray area can confuse the best of them, especially the perfectionists. With mastery and evolution of soul, perfectionists become much more tolerant of themselves, which translates into being more tolerant of others, which translates into a more relaxed approach to life, thereby overcoming challenge and facilitating the creation of the conditions for self-love and joy. Problem-solving takes on additional flavors during the mastery journey—lending more color, vibrancy, and choices when problem-solving. It increases the momentum of successful resolution by providing a greater view of choices and a more tolerable process. It also fosters a mindset where excellence and perfection are not synonymous, so internal conflict is minimized, and shorter time lags are experienced from start to finish.

- It is not uncommon for other people's opinions and mandates to drive decisions and create a wet blanket to have to live under. It's cold and uncomfortable. Obligations can specialize into areas outside what's ethically and lovingly necessary and flow into areas that cause great burdens and unwarranted stress. As the self-mastery journey progresses, it's common that an individual has an easier time saying no. The level of thought and emotion attributed to what other people think of a person has less gravity, and because in mastery there is a genuine understanding of how to be true to the self, motivations are primarily driven internally instead of externally. Simply put, with time and self-mastery, a person doesn't care as much about what people think, but they care deeply about the level of joy that people, places, and events bring to their quality of life and vice versa.

- A person who is on the self-mastery journey usually feels healthier than they did before, and they can even look younger than they used to, aging gracefully. The relationship with healthy thoughts, food, exercise, and overall activities of healthy living resides more frequently in the autopilot category because the higher self is more engaged than the human ego and fosters a higher vibration of consciousness. This enrichment of consciousness continues with time, and food challenges, for example, decrease in number and rate of recurrence. The love of self provides great freedom.

- An individual has fewer agendas—especially hidden. Motives become more loving and transparent on the self-mastery journey because there is an overwhelming sense that there's nothing to hide. When a person lives life in the highest good of themselves and others, their agenda is usually fairly clear for everyone to see. It is one of the manifestations of the self-mastery journey that is frequently noted by others, especially in the workplace and in family dynamics.

- In mastery, the many faces of fear reduce exponentially with soul growth. There is a greater sensitivity to the onset and presence of fear and the skill set to minimize or eliminate fear matures throughout the journey. With mastery, when fear presents, it can be recognized immediately, and an individual can use the plethora of internal tools to change their perspective from fear based to love or freedom based. The rate limiting steps to traverse from fear to love continues to be minimized with practice.

- An individual will notice it takes them longer to get angry and much less time to get over things. The fuse gets longer, and it seems like there are fewer situations and people to forgive. This is partly attributable to the fact that the mastery journey allows an individual to really understand that everything a person says and does is a reflection of what goes on inside of them. When a person understands this essential element of human behavior, they do not take things personally. When words or actions are not taken personally, there are far fewer circumstances that can upset the apple cart; therefore, fewer apples to pick up and reorganize and less forgiveness is necessitated. It's really important for everyone to realize that each person is a product of so many elements of living—exposure to everyone and everything—people, places, and events. Given the level of consciousness where people reside, they generally do the best they can given the dataset and internal level of mastery they have attained. There is so much to making a human—not only from the lifetime in which they currently reside, but also a great deal of history and learning from other lifetimes and dimensions. Nobody will ever know the path of another—even the people themselves often have wounds from a past they didn't realize existed.

- With the love of self and evolution of soul comes the realization of more beauty within. When beauty within is acknowledged, external beauty becomes more evident and vibrant. Everything is more beautiful with love. People become more beautiful—even the recognition of human frailty that resides in everyone takes on a greater level of preciousness through the eyes and spirit of one who traverses the self-mastery journey. The earth takes on more beauty, and nature becomes a pillar of strength to assist in traversing life's challenges. Just knowing you can go outside and smell the freshness of the air and feel the freedom of the breeze is motivating, captivating, and strengthening.

- As the mastery journey brings a vibrancy and peace to life, the humor of situations and events become more easily visible. As an individual cuts more slack for themselves and others because tolerance for human frailty increases, humor appears to replace former avenues of frustration and anger. When a person takes themselves more lightly, they can more easily laugh at blunders and errors. The world can be a very funny place.

- As the mastery journey continues and our hearts overflow with more love each day, the love of self that is enriched creates the conditions for a heightened awareness, love, and compassion for all things. This love casts a shadow of beauty on all that is, deepening a feeling of Oneness with all. This feeling of Oneness can be the fuel that creates a fire of love whose ambers spread to everyone it encounters, thereby creating the conditions for a love, joy, and peace-filled life. Among the chaos will reside the peace and resiliency that carries an individual through the toughest of times and elevates the joy of the best of times.

- The most treasured and noticeable gifts when traversing the self-mastery journey is the beautiful budding of love and all kinds of coping and de-stressing mechanisms that reside within our internal toolbox. Within the self, there is a growing and incredible peace. Self-awareness and self-actualization enhance the innate ability to understand connections—connections that affect everything and anything. It is the sincere acceptance and understanding of all the synchronicities of life that underscore the presence of connections. From the connections within the body of the energy network that works with our physical, mental, emotional, and spiritual being to assist us to heal our human mind and body, to the connections that elevate our spirits, all offer continual divine communication and resonance with our Source. The knowing and understanding of Oneness truly awakens the self. This awakening is what everyone is searching for—whether they comprehend it or not.

- As the journey progresses, the Oneness is more deeply recognized and felt, and this Oneness is given the opportunity by the conceding human ego to dominate our lives through our thoughts, intentions, and actions. Our eyes will see through the grace of Oneness, our ears will hear through the grace of Oneness, and every step we take will be illuminated by Oneness. As we walk hand in hand with the I AM presence of the self, our Creator and all that is divine, by the grace of the Holy Spirit and Oneness, life will be beautiful. Just remember, a beautiful and joy-filled life is not devoid of challenge, obstacles, loss, or sadness. It is beautiful because we understand who we are, what we are, where we are, and why we are . . . and when this lifetime is complete and our soul has spent the perfect amount of time on planet earth (because no matter how long or short, it's always the perfect amount of time), the mind, body, and spirit will witness that love commands the universe, that we are created from and by unconditional love, and all we need and want is waiting for us back home.

Chapter Eighteen

The Celebration of YOU

A quote often attributed to Mark Twain is, "The two most important days in your life are the day you were born and the day you find out why." We were made in the image of our Creator, and that image is love. The threads of love are intertwined in all that sustains itself within the life force and consciousness that knows no death. We decided to come to earth to partake in the good, bad, and the ugly. The land of learning, testing, and density, we selected our parents, our family, and those who would play an integral role in assisting us to bring our co-created plans to fruition. We didn't accept the challenge of being comfortable all the time. We accepted the challenge to grow, learn, and evolve in mind and spirit. We accepted the challenge to assist our soul in attaining the highest vibration of love possible, expanding closer and closer to the consciousness of God. Be proud of all your accomplishments from learning your alphabet onward. You read this book for a reason. I hope the reason is the love you either have or want to have for yourself and the world around you. You can make the world a better place by loving who you are and helping others see the beauty and divinity within themselves. With every thought and every step, be love.

Transitions of hope are part of life. Hope brings joy

to life, clarity among the clouds, and glimmers of light to all levels of darkness. Hope, love, and gratitude are powerful forces that help us navigate through challenges. When you become adept at recognizing the many faces of fear that manifest from moment to moment in life, use all the self-mastery tools you've developed to replace that fear with love. Love creates freedom to exist without the shackles that impede growth, happiness, contentment, and joy.

I have several T-shirts I love to wear in various colors that say, *"Running on Hope."* I purchased them from the Brave Like Gabe foundation. I never knew Gabe, but I love her. Gabriele Grunewald was a professional middle-distance runner who represented the US at numerous championships. She died when she was thirty-two-years old from a rare type of cancer called adenoid cystic carcinoma. During treatments and after numerous surgeries, she remained a beacon of love and hope for the world. She never gave up, and she allowed her surgical scars to remain visible during her runs and races. She may have succumbed to cancer, but she never succumbed to negativity, pessimism, or victimization. She was a relentless optimist who did everything she could to bring awareness of cancer with strength, resilience, and hope. Her advocacy lives on, and she is just one shining example of how devastation was overcome with love and positivity. I run on hope. I live on hope—and so does everyone else. Hope is the light at the end of every tunnel. Hope is the silver lining in every cloud. Hope is a beautiful manifestation of love.

May the everlasting love and light of all that is divine envelop you today and all the days of your life, so that you may be well prepared to bathe in the unconditional love of our Creator forevermore. May you know the truth of love. May you always be in love, and when it slips your mind that you are love, may you turn things around so you'll be reminded, once again, to be love. Love will put everything in tune and allow for harmony.

I hope that we can all love living love and love being love, for that is how our world will become a better place, one person at a time, from the inside out.

Thank you for taking this journey with me—I truly <u>hope</u> it was a valuable use of your time. Much love to all.

—*Mare*

About the Author

Maryann Roefaro is a highly intuitive spiritual mentor and well-respected leader in the Central New York Community. Dedicating her career to healthcare, she retired after 45 years of experience, over 35 of which included executive leadership positions. Spending 23 years as the CEO of Hematology-Oncology Associates of CNY, she retired in February of 2025.

Maryann believes that every relationship we have begins with the relationship we have with ourselves. Committed to her own self-mastery journey, her motto is to help make the world a better place, one person at a time, from the inside-out. With this intention in her heart, *Transitions of Hope* is her fourth publication, the others being, *Building the Team from the Inside-Out, A Human's Purpose by Millie the Dog, and Snippets from the Inside-Out by Millie the Dog.* She maintains an active role in leadership and spiritual development through various speaking engagements and her podcast, Transitions of Hope.

Maryann received a Doctor of Divinity degree from the American Institute of Holistic Theology, a Master of Science degree from Upstate Medical University and a Bachelor of Science degree from Albany College of Pharmacy. She is an ordained minister through Metaphysical Universal Ministries, a certified Heart Centered Hypnotherapist, a Reiki Master/Teacher and a certified ChiRunning/ChiWalking instructor.

Maryann has served and continues to serve on many community boards, including many non-profit organizations. She is the co-founder of CancerConnects, Inc. and to date, remains the organization's Board President.

Maryann is married to Tom Carranti and has two daughters, two step-sons, and 6 beautiful grandchildren. Two precious souls that have captured Maryann's hearts for all eternity are Mille and Bella. Millie is a mini poodle, and Bella is a medium labradoodle. They are beautiful souls whose unconditional love bring her great joy and peace. Bella was Maryann's former husband Dale Franz's pup and she was blessed to adopt her during his illness and transition to the realm of pure love.

Other Books by Maryann Roefaro

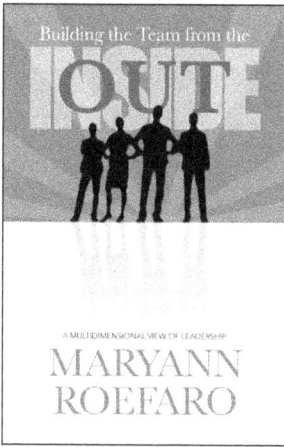

Building the Team from the Inside Out
by Maryann Roefaro

Building the Team from the Inside Out is a powerful leadership book that overflows with concepts and philosophies that will build winning teams and create a happier and more personally fulfilled and enlightened life. This book is a recipe for self-mastery that Maryann intuitively inserts into the workplace. Any and every leader with an open mind should read this treasure. She believes that every relationship we have begins with the one we have with our self. She has proven that the success and harmony of any work group or corporation is dependent on the mastery and resilience of its individual parts. Join Maryann on a journey of leadership development, proven throughout 35 years of executive leadership experience that will change the way you look at challenge, adversity, and the interconnectedness of people.

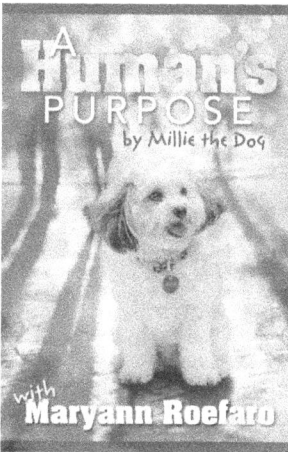

A Humans Purpose
by Millie the Dog
with Maryann Roefaro

This book is for anyone searching for the deeper meanings in life and death. It is for those on a spiritual path who want to understand themselves and others more profoundly. Millie is an old soul that will steal your heart and help open your mind to new ideas and concepts that will allow for a greater infusion of love into all aspects of your being. This book can help a person create the conditions for a love and joy filled life. Millie would love to accompany you on your self-mastery journey!

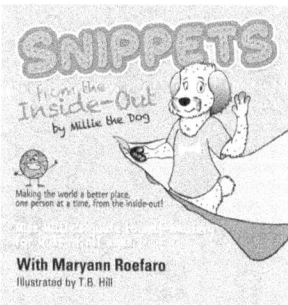

Snippets from the Inside-Out
by Millie the Dog
with Maryann Rocfaro

Making the world a better place, one person at a time, from the inside-out! Miss Millie's guide to self-mastery for kids of all ages.

Available on Amazon

www.ingramcontent.com/pod-product-compliance
Lightning Source LLC
Chambersburg PA
CBHW021050090426
42738CB00006B/272